GO WEST

10 Principles that Guided
My Cowboy Journey

JEREMY SPARKS

with **STEPHEN CALDWELL**

"*Go West* is the inspirational story of a tough and faith-based cowboy who teaches the reader how to 'shoot the gap' like a bullfighter in life, love, and faith."

C.J. Box
No. 1 *New York Times* Bestselling Author, *Off the Grid*

"Jeremy Sparks made a commitment to serve his country, and made a commitment to himself to serve God. His 10 principles can help anyone struggling with personal and professional balance. *Go West* is a must-read for us all."

Flint Rasmussen
Professional Bull Riders, Exclusive Entertainer

"Jeremy Sparks witnesses to the rawness of rodeo bullfighting and the reality of God's calling in *Go West*. Sparks' story of passion, struggle, and commitment demonstrates that God has a plan, and, when we stray, there is always a path back."

Michael J. Carey
Major General, USAF (Retired)

"Jeremy's journey is uplifting and inspiring! In *Go West*, Jeremy proves that, with God, the possibilities are endless."

Jake Barnes
Seven-time World Champion Team Roper

"*Go West* is a remarkable true story of a man with faith that overcomes the obstacles of life and makes a difference in the world around him!"

Clay O'Brien Cooper
Seven-time World Champion Team Roper

"*Go West* is not only an entertaining read, but also one that provides you with a transferable skill set based on 10 principles for thriving in this world. No matter who you are or what you do, using and honing these skills will help you achieve more than you ever thought possible."

Fran Smith
Book Publishing Director, *Western Horseman Magazine*

"If you want to be a champion in life, *Go West* is the book for you. I encourage all to read Sparks' incredible journey in discovering his true calling."

Scott Mendes
World Champion Bull Rider,
Founder of Western Harvest Ministries

"Jeremy Sparks has done what few before him have—served his country while still responding to God's call to Go West—'Witnessing, Encouraging, Serving, and Testifying'—as a rodeo bullfighter. *Go West* will leave readers with a strong conviction to follow God's lead."

Karl Stressman
Commissioner, Professional Rodeo Cowboys Association

"*Go West* is a compelling novel about the perseverance of a young officer and bullfighter who taught a reluctant Air Force leadership to not only support his rodeo ambitions, but to sponsor him. The U.S. Air Force core values—Integrity First/Service Before Self/Excellence In All We Do—rings loud throughout the pages of *Go West*. Beyond inspiring."

James Carroll
Brigadier General (Retired), USAF

"This is an excellent story of dreams, setbacks, commitment, forgiveness, and, most of all, great faith. Inspiring and insightful. It makes you think about your own life in a different way—a better way."

Bob Budd

Chairman, Cheyenne Frontier Days

"If you want to read an unbelievable story of setbacks, heartache, redemption, and hope, *Go West* is for you. Jeremy Sparks shares his fascinating life story in a compelling way that shows the change that Jesus can bring into a person's life."

Dr. Nick Floyd

Teaching Pastor, Cross Church, Fayetteville, Arkansas

"I watched the courage, dedication, and skill of Jeremy Sparks at the Cheyenne Frontier Days rodeo all nine years he performed. *Go West* is a true reflection of the man. He is the real deal!"

Marty LaVor

Author, *No Bull!*

"Each and every bullfighter has a life unlike any other profession. It is grueling, dangerous, painful, and highly satisfying to those who make it a living. Jeremy Sparks has conveyed his experiences with the ability few others in this profession have. His time in the arena was inspired by God, and his life was meant to guide and encourage others to achieve more than they ever imagined, regardless of background, education, or direction in life. *Go West* is a must read!"

Gail Woerner

Rodeo Historian and Author, *Fearless Funnymen*

"Jeremy Sparks truly encourages us to live a better life through sharing the gospel. His passion, encouragement, and commitment are evident when reading *Go West*. Sparks' message is one that will speak to the cowboy spirit in all of us."

John Contos
Board of Directors, Cheyenne Frontier Days

"Jeremy Sparks provides the insights and secret sauce of how he defied the odds and made his dream become a reality. *Go West* explains the power and potential of having a challenging life plan, a family's support, true friends, unswerving dedication, and unbreakable faith. Read *Go West*, get inspired to 'Cowboy Up,' and actualize your dream."

Ed Fienga
Brigadier General, USAF (Retired)

"A behind-the-chutes look into the world of a professional rodeo bullfighter with the tremendous passion and relentless determination it takes to overcome mental, physical, and emotional adversity while balancing faith, family, and life choices. Jeremy Sparks instills in the reader that with intensive goal setting, courage, sacrifice, and conviction to God, all things are possible. *Go West* offers a message that inspires you to chase your dreams and become better in all facets of your life."

Al Sandvold
National Finals Rodeo, Wrangler Bullfight Qualifier

"*Go West* is a knockout! An awesome story of one man who fulfills his childhood dream to serve as a rodeo bullfighter protecting cowboys and entertaining people around the world."

Bob Romer
"The Bull Dancer," National Finals Rodeo Bullfighter

"Whether serving his country, fighting bulls, or raising his family, Jeremy Sparks has shown that by 'walking the walk,' his Christian values lights his path of life. *Go West* will be a guiding light for folks of all ages."

Max Maxfield
Wyoming Secretary of State (Retired)

"Jeremy Sparks is a top-notch bullfighter and an even better person. His inspired journey will captivate *Go West* readers from the start. By the time he heads to one last rodeo, you'll have a whole new appreciation for cowboy lifesavers."

Kyle Partain
Rodeo Columnist, *Western Horseman Magazine*

"*Go West* is inspiring story of how a young man's dreams became a reality through self-sacrifice, sheer determination, and a strong commitment to his faith. Jeremy Sparks' life story is proof that through faith you can achieve great things."

Rod Hottle
Colonel, USAF (Retired), Board of Directors,
Cheyenne Frontier Days

"An amazing story of trials, tribulations, hurt, and failures resolved through determination and faith. *Go West* reinforces that having God as your 'spotter' is a game plan for success!"

Darin Westby
General Chairman, Cheyenne Frontier Days Committee

"Jeremy Sparks, in *Go West*, shares his life as a small town boy growing up to becoming a member of the Cheyenne Frontier Days Rodeo Hall of Fame. *Go West* is a fascinating look into a world unknown to many."

Dr. Karla Hughes
Chancellor, University of Arkansas-Monticello

"If you are seeking God's best for your life, but find yourself in a difficult season, do yourself a favor and read *Go West*."

Ted Cunningham
Pastor, Woodland Hills Family Church, Branson, Missouri,
Author, *Fun Loving You*

"Written from the heart, Sparks' book is a testament to the journey that led a young man to the greatest arenas in professional rodeo. *Go West* bears witness to the hope, courage, and deep faith that guided Sparks through trials that would have stopped an ordinary man in his tracks. At its core, *Go West* is a deep exploration of how one man's relationship with his God helped him prevail in the most challenge arena of all: life."

Mike Kassel
Deputy Director, Old West Museum, Cheyenne, Wyoming

"In *Go West*, Jeremy shares his journey to become a Hall of Fame bullfighter and shines a bright light on the calling that brought him there."

Scottie L. Zamzow
Colonel USAF, Former Lead Soloist USAF Thunderbird Pilot

"*Go West* is an honest look at the United States Air Force's only professional bullfighter's struggles, courage, and determination to follow his dream under God's lead."

Dwayne Hargo
World Champion Bullfighter

"*Go West* is a rare find. An honest account of Jeremy Sparks' life as he follows God's call for his life. It shows us that if we walk with God, we can realize our dreams."

Kent Sturman
Director, ProRodeo Hall of Fame

"Jeremy Sparks' *Go West* lets you into the mind of a rodeo star. It's a true testament to his faith and a glimpse into what empowered him to step in front of untamed rage."

Chad Eubank
Champion All-Around Cowboy

"You might ask, 'What would a rodeo bullfighter have to say that I could find useful in my life?' We could all use a person with Jeremy Sparks' mindfulness and perception in our life. Everyone needs to know these 10 cowboy principles."

Dr. Jim Lugg
World Renowned Urologist, Surgeon, Lecturer

GO WEST

*10 Principles that Guided
My Cowboy Journey*

BY JEREMY SPARKS
WITH STEPHEN CALDWELL

Dedication

For Elmer and Claudie Cruce Sparks: Fighting bulls pales in comparison to your courageous fights with cancer.

Thanks for the fearless example and encouraging me to bite off more than I could chew...and chew it.

Until we meet again,

I love you, Mom and Dad.

CONTENTS

Foreword

JEREMY SPARKS, THE COWBOY SOLDIER

By Justin McKee
Rodeo Television Personality

I have always said that cowboys and soldiers have a lot in common: Both love the flag and their country. Both respect their elders and history. Both will rush to a neighbor's aid. And both are willing to lay down their life for a fellow man.

As a rodeo announcer for more than 20 years, I've seen a lot of great cowboys and one extremely fine cowboy soldier—Jeremy Sparks.

It takes guts to be a soldier, and it takes guts to be a cowboy. I believe these rare breeds are a great example of what the rest of America should aspire to.

Perhaps it's an attitude of confidence. Cowboys and soldiers know where they come from—their legacy, their lineage, and their traditions. This insight helps them prepare for and embrace the future, no matter what it may entail.

In short, the same confidence of soldiers and cowboys leads to peace. And isn't that what we are all really seeking? The confidence of knowing who we are and why we exist on this earth will get us what everyone is looking for: real peace.

As *Go West* explains, peace comes from having the right perspective. Life is all about how we look at things. If we look at the negative, we're going to get the negative. But if we walk around with a thankful spirit and a constant attitude of prayer and thanksgiving, we're going to walk in abundance.

Jeremy has walked down many roads. Some were dead ends. And some led to a destiny that made his dreams come true. But whichever road he took, he gained life experiences and learned to grow into a God-given perspective.

His storytelling ability truly draws you in and makes you feel like you were with him as he was growing up, serving his country, and saving cowboys as a rodeo bullfighter.

These athletes are different from the traditional matadors who risk their lives using a cape and sword. Bullfighters risk life and limb, too, but for different reasons and with different outcomes. They have no cape or sword, and they don't kill the bull when the show is over. Instead, rodeo bullfighters selflessly protect other cowboys.

Bulls are aggressive and, many times, downright mean. When a rodeo bull rider gets thrown to the ground by a bull that wants to mow him over, bullfighters step right in front of the bull's face. It's not a death wish; it's to divert the bull's attention from the fallen rider. Throughout Jeremy's career, I've witnessed him swoop in like a superhero with savvy, bravery, and athleticism to save the day… and his fellow cowboy.

So let's be clear: He wasn't a rodeo clown. Clowns tell jokes to entertain the crowd. He was a bullfighter, the very ones risking their lives to protect bull riders who have been thrown from an angry bull. They're the secret service of rodeo; it's no laughing matter.

In bullfighting, if you hide and deny your weaknesses, you may very well die. Faced with that reality, Jeremy embraced self-awareness and learned from his weaknesses. The same approach applies to life.

Rick Warren, author of A *Purpose Driven Life*, said, "We can impress people by talking about our successes, but we will IMPACT people when we admit our failures and weaknesses and point them to God who can work a miracle out of their mess."

Get ready to experience 10 powerful life principles and learn firsthand how God turned Jeremy's sometimes messy life into a powerful and inspiring message about how God can lead cowboys, soldiers, and anyone else coming to Him with a willing heart—including you.

Bull's Eye

Flying in to rescue a fleeting bull rider at the 2006 "Daddy of 'Em All."

Photo by Eva Scofield

INTRODUCTION

I was born a dreamer.

That's not unusual, of course. Most of us dream, especially when we're young. And there was nothing extraordinary about most of my dreams as a child—that is, until January 20, 1991.

That's the day everything changed.

That's the day my dream became my destiny.

I was only 13 when I first heard God speak the plans for my future. It wasn't a conviction, a feeling, or a thought. It was, without a doubt, God revealing a sneak peek of His plans for my life. The experience remains just as clear today as it was 25 years ago.

I know that might sound mystical and strange, perhaps even unbelievable. Does God really speak to people these days? And if He does, why would He choose a lowly teenager living in Middle-of-Nowhere, Arkansas?

Trust me, I wish I knew the answers to those questions. There was, and is, nothing special about me. So I don't know the "why me." But I believe this: God speaks to all of us in some way or another. And if we listen and obey, He will use us—somehow or other—to bring glory to His name.

I was praying as I sat in my bedroom in our home just south of Fountain Hill, Arkansas. My palms became sweaty, my heart raced, and my entire body quivered uncontrollably. I didn't fully understand the magnitude of what was happening. So I quieted myself and embraced the Holy Spirit's presence.

In that moment, God placed a dream in my heart and spoke to my soul: "You will go out to witness, encourage, serve, and testify."

That was the meat of it, the part that's burned into my memory like a brand in the backside of an open range steer. I couldn't run from it or deny it, but I also had no idea what to do with it.

Go where? Witness to whom? Encourage and serve whom? Testify about what? When? How?

Within a few months, however, God's call on my life became abundantly clear. And with the faith of a child, I boldly promised myself I would achieve this God-given dream by becoming a professional rodeo bullfighter.

Some boys want to become doctors. Others want to become football stars or play the hero in movies.

I wanted to be a cowboy.

That might sound like a childhood fantasy. I knew the moment God spoke to me, however, that I was destined to Go West as a rodeo bullfighter. By Go West, I don't just mean that I was to go in that direction or that I was to metaphorically go into the great unknown like the early settlers. Both of those things are true. But I felt called to "Get Out, Witness, Encourage, Serve, and Testify" as I crisscrossed the country—to GO WEST.

Having received a specific vision, I realized I had been given a unique gift. So I devoted my life to establishing goals that served as milestones, marking my path to completion. Yet, quickly, the path became a journey—a long, hard, peaks-and-valleys type of adventure.

Along the way, I sacrificed, bled, cried, and nearly died. While I continued to listen to God, I didn't always obey. But I never quit.

I had no backup—not even a Plan B.

So off I went, a kid with a God-given dream from the Land of Opportunity, longing to *Go West*, where cowboys drift and live free or die.

THE DAY SPARKS FLEW

I'm hot. My skin is tingling, I can't move, I can't feel, and I can't see.

I'm lying motionless in a small pool of water that has collected on a hard, hot, and nasty dirt floor.

It's 105 degrees, and I can't regain consciousness. I need ice. Water. Anything to help cool my body. I know I need to get up, but I can't move.

My journey had abruptly stopped under the hot, southern summer sun. It was over. My body lay lifeless in a puddle of nasty, stale water.

It had happened in a flash.

There were only average-sounding crackles and pops, not a big bang or a loud scream. Just a little sizzle and a few sparks, but that was enough to knock me backward seven feet before I landed on my side.

I had merely plugged an industrial fan into an electrical outlet. Nothing unusual or risky about that. I was working on a tomato farm that summer. The tomato shed had a roof, but no walls, so parts of it were shaded depending on the path of the sun. But without a breeze, the lingering heat made for miserable working conditions. I was turning on the fan hoping to cool everyone working in the shed.

Unbeknownst to me, the cord had been cut since the last time we'd used the fan. The exposed portion was lying in a puddle of water nearly 50 feet away. Just below the outlet, however, the end piece rested unassuming. There was no sign of danger. But when I inserted the plug into the outlet, it shorted and sent a wave of electricity throughout my body. The 220 volts sizzled me like a piece of bacon in my momma's frying pan.

I was only 18, and my adventure hadn't even really begun. A few months earlier, I had accepted a scholarship to compete for the rodeo team at McNeese State University, but it was summer and I was still in Arkansas working on the tomato farm. I had planned to earn some spending money, breeze through college, and head west to win shiny rodeo belt buckles and championship titles.

Now it was all ending before it had begun. Death lingered.

Taking the jolt from a 220-volt outlet while standing in water created just the right amount of current to knock me down and dislodge the power cord from my hand. Sparks flew. Never before had my name been such an accurate description of my life. Sparks literally flew!

I can't quit, I told myself. *I can't die.*

Using all the mental strength and intestinal fortitude I could muster, I fought to stay alive.

"Help! Jeremy is out!" someone said.

I could faintly hear the words that seemed to come from at least a mile away. The voices grew louder and the words slowly started to run together, but I could only hear chaos. I sensed that people were gathering around me.

"Do something!" another shouted.

My skin was tingling, but I still couldn't move. People were getting concerned, yet I remained lifeless on the dirt floor.

"He's just playing. Get back to work," said James Meeks, the boss man.

I had been known to pull pretty good pranks while on the clock. Just two days earlier, I had caught a bull snake and buried it with ripe tomatoes in a five-gallon bucket. You can imagine what happened when a lady emptied the bucket onto a conveyer belt. So I couldn't blame anyone for considering it another prank.

It certainly was no joke. But who knew? And this time I couldn't defend myself. I couldn't even communicate what had just transpired.

"Pour some water on him," James said to another worker. "That will get him up."

I started to squirm a little and tried to talk, but my words didn't have the slightest volume. Inside my head, I was yelling. Outside my mouth, there wasn't the faintest sound.

"I'm hurt," I tried to yell. "I'm hurt."

Not a sound. I continued to lay blistering in the summer heat, the sun beaming in on me. It seemed like a lifetime had passed since the first yell for help. In reality, it had only been a couple of minutes. But those minutes were precious to my survival. If I was going to fulfill my God-given dream, I needed a miracle.

Oh God, don't hide your face from me now. Hear my prayer!

My eyesight began to get a little stronger—blurry still, but I could see motions. I made out a shape standing over me that appeared to be James. The boss was holding what turned out to be a pitcher of water. As he tilted it toward me, the words I had been screaming finally found some volume.

"I am hurt," I yelled with slurred speech as the water plummeted onto my head.

Like a phoenix rising from the ashes, I stretched my hand toward the sky and stated the facts. It was a simple but pointed recollection.

"I've been electrocuted," I said in desperation.

A few good things happened when the water hit me. First, people finally realized this was a real-world emergency. All jokes were off the table. Second, the water cooled me down a touch, washing away the sweat that had been steadily rolling off of my body.

"Get the truck!" James said, a sense of urgency now in his booming voice. "Hurry, we've got to get him to the emergency room!"

I'm not sure who he was yelling at, and perhaps he wasn't either, but a truck arrived promptly.

We were deep in rural south Arkansas. Pumping Station Road

in Ashley County to be exact. It was 1995, and cellphones hadn't made their way to this part of the Delta just yet. Even if someone had owned a high-tech "bag phone," reception would have been another issue. We were so remote, sunlight had to be piped in. Simply put, it was quicker to get me to the emergency room in the farm truck than to get an ambulance to the farm and then back to an ER.

I would like to have heard the conversation if an ambulance had been called. Getting the directions relayed would have been one giant feat. Having the ambulance actually find us would have been another!

I imagine it would have gone something like this:

James: "Y'all, we have a farm hand down. Send help."

Dispatch: "Sir, what is wrong?"

James: "Good question. We don't know."

Dispatch: "Have you asked him where he hurts?"

James: "Yes. All he has said was that he was electrocuted."

Dispatch: "Sir, where are you?"

James: "6.8 miles south of Fountain Hill. You need to head north on Highway 133. Go about 17 miles and turn left. There should be a white house right there where you need to turn. Go over the train tracks. Keep going and the road will appear to end. Don't worry, keep straight. The road will turn from blacktop to dirt. Keep straight. You should be in the middle of a tomato field in no time at all. Look to your left about the time you lose faith in these directions, and we'll be standing out there waiting on you. I'll be wearing Big Smith overalls and a straw hat."

Needless to say, I was thankful for the farm truck.

When the truck arrived, a few co-workers picked me up and slid me onto the passenger seat. I was dazed and slightly confused, but it felt good to be out of the hot, stale, nasty water.

My hands were hurting something fierce and I couldn't figure out why. I didn't know it at the time, but apparently I had urinated on myself shortly after the accident. The fact that no one seemed to notice or care was just another sign that this wasn't a laughing matter. Any other time, I wouldn't have heard the end of that.

The speed limit on Highway 133 was 55 miles per hour. But with the flashers on, James behind the wheel, and me lying lifeless riding shotgun, Highway 133 transformed into the Arkansas Autobahn.

James and I were good buddies who shared a mutual respect for one another. Even though he was the boss and I was a worker, my parents had instilled in me a set of core values that he appreciated. And James was a good boss. He was always fair, even appreciating a good joke and prank every now and then.

I slipped in and out of consciousness as we sped toward help. James lost count of how many times I blacked out and vomited, but it was clear he was distraught by the severity of my condition. Not only did he have to get me to help, he also knew he would have the eventual duty of calling my parents. In an attempt to stay strong, James tried to throw out a few jokes, but I was too weak and incoherent to engage or be amused.

I began to black out every few minutes. At times, it lasted a few seconds and others I'd be out longer. When I awoke the last time, I was lying on a hospital table and nurses were cutting off my jeans. I could hear faint voices and, though my vision was still blurry, I could see workers feverishly situating equipment.

When I noticed the shock paddles were on a push cart next to my gurney, I panicked. And when the doctor instructed, "Have the defibrillator in place and be ready should he code," I wet myself again.

These are my city jeans they're cutting off!

Strange what goes through your mind at a time like that, but they were Guess Jeans! And growing up in the country, I didn't have many "city jeans" to wear. My closet housed one pair, and for some unknown reason I had decided to wear them to work that day. My one pair of "city jeans" became my only pair of "city shorts!"

My focus quickly shifted from the superficial issue of my pants to the profound topic of my survival. I began to worry about my next breath, next minute, next hour, and next day. Then it happened.

I flatlined—no heartbeat, no natural breath.

Thankfully, it lasted only long enough for God to breathe life back into my body.

I'm not sure what code the doctors called my condition. But my parents received a printout of the EKG when they arrived, and the piece of paper showed a flat line stretching several inches long. It was enough to terrify my parents, concern the doctors, and prove to me that God was in control.

Momma always said God takes care of fools and babies. I'm not sure which category I fit into that day, but God saw me through the accident. Fool or baby, I was happy to be alive.

MY COWBOY JOURNEY

Being electrocuted didn't knock my God-given dream out of my body, nor did it weaken my resolve. It was simply a course correction at the will of God.

At 18, I stood at my first major fork in the road. My journey was just getting started and only God knew the route. I had only one plan, which was to trust Him.

Oswald Chambers once said, "Trust God and do the next thing." So I pushed forward, never giving up on what I believed to be my destiny. And while I failed Him many times, God never let me down.

This is the story of my cowboy journey and the principles that carried me along the way. While some are Biblical truths instilled by my parents, others were learned while pursuing my dream. Unfortunately, it took drifting off the beaten path from time to time to truly understand their importance.

I believe they are foundational in any journey, whether you're fighting bulls in a rodeo, navigating bull-headed coworkers over office politics, or trying to wrangle mischievous teenagers.

These are the principles I'll unpack as I share my story, and I believe they'll serve you well as you respond to God's call in your life—whatever it is and however He speaks to you:

- Lend a Hand—Exhortation can change a life.

- Step Through—Faith makes all things possible.

- Bear Down—The hard work of preparation never ends.

- Shoot the Gap—To sacrifice is to live.

- EGO (Edging God Out)—Humility is a true reflection of strength.

- Cowboy Up—Know your priorities.

- The Razor—Confidence is a fine line.

- The Gold Buckle—Integrity can't be bought.

- Find Your Spotter—Listen to smart people.

- Turn 'Em Out—Restoration leads to fulfillment.

I was an ordinary kid who eventually lived out my passion for the Western way of life and a God-given vision by becoming a professional bullfighter. So I'm living proof that even a small-town kid has big-time potential.

The road wasn't straight and the path wasn't easy. Along the way, I overcame the near-death experience from that electrical shock, suffered multiple concussions from too-close encounters with bulls, and endured a bitter divorce and international child-custody battle. I looked fear in the eyes and refused to blink, proudly serving in the military following the terrorist attacks on 9/11. And, eventually, I became the youngest cowboy enshrined in the Cheyenne Frontier Days Hall of Fame.

Through all of the highs and lows, these principles guided me along my cowboy journey. They never let me down…when I applied them. So I hope by sharing my story, you can learn from my mistakes and successes and apply these principles to your life. Because if God can use me, I know He can use you!

The Perfect Save

Shooting the gap to save a cowboy at the 2006 Cheyenne Frontier Days.

Rodeo in Cheyenne, Wyoming.

Photo by Tony Bruguiere

SECTION ONE
A Cowboy's Calling

chapter 1
MY GOD-GIVEN VISION

The stare down between man and beast is the ultimate battle of survival. After 70 dreadful seconds, a winner emerges. And a loser, if he's fortunate, walks away.

It's the modern-day gladiator sport of American freestyle bull-fighting.

Outmatched in size, speed, and strength, it appears unfair for a man to look death in the eyes like this. And that's why so few men do it—and why even fewer do it for very long.

Yet, there I was.

It was March 2000, and I was standing in the middle of a dirt-covered arena floor in Lawton, Oklahoma. George Thorogood and The Destroyers were belting *Bad to the Bone* through the stadium speakers all around me. Adrenaline rushed as my heart beat 180 times per minute.

This wasn't my first rodeo, as the saying goes, but it was my first freestyle bullfight of this caliber. It was one of the most respected events of the year, the Rex Dunn Invitational, and it took me from the minor leagues to the majors.

In reality, it was my first time to fight on the big stage. In baseball terms, I had made it to The Show. Now I just had to avoid being killed off.

With a quick motion of the hand, I signaled to start the fight, and then I heard the command from the arena announcer.

"Turn 'em out," he yelled.

The bull weighed in at 1,800 pounds. He was high-headed, wild, mean, and appropriately called "Nasty."

His reputation preceded him. Before the fight ever started, guys in the locker room had shared the story of Nasty near-fatally injuring his last opponent.

"Only one guy has walked out on his own terms," said Rex Dunn himself, legendary bullfighter and Nasty's owner.

He paused as a mischievous smile overtook his face.

Not exactly what I wanted to hear.

I'd eaten very little that day. Nerves and excitement had spoiled my appetite. A garden salad and a sweet tea for lunch were the extent of it. Still, I felt ready. I'd trained most of my life for this moment. And now it was here.

As Nasty sprinted to my position in the middle of the arena, I started to run toward him. My goal: Engage him. Dance with him, if you will. But don't get killed by him. The first point of contact between bull and fighter typically establishes the tone of the fight. So I braced for the worst, but expected the best. I faked as if going to the left, throwing all of my weight in that direction.

Nasty took the fake.

I stopped in mid-stride, transitioning to the right as he flew by. His horn had missed my ribs by a fraction of an inch.

Whew, I thought, *that was a close one.*

The fight was on.

For the next 50 seconds, Nasty turned me every which way but loose. One moment I was flung through the air, the next I was pinned to the ground beneath Nasty's two massive horns.

With every hit, the crowd let out an audible gasp.

Like a boxer knocked down by a blow to the head, there was a choice to make: Stand up or surrender.

With every pass, my life flashed before my eyes.

"Get up, Jeremy," I told myself. "You weren't called to quit."

My knees were busted and bleeding, and my clothes were completely shredded. Hydrated by only sweet tea, my body began to shut down.

Fear set in as the fight came to a close.

"How much noise can you make for Jeremy Sparks?!" the announcer beckoned.

The thunderous cheers fell on deaf ears. I would have preferred air to the applause.

Nasty won again.

The ambulance rushed me to the emergency room. As we neared the hospital, I asked one of the medical technicians to call my momma.

"She'll be worried if she doesn't hear from me after the event," I told him.

"Momma, the bullfight is over," I said bluntly as soon as she picked up the call. "I'm okay, just pulling into the hospital. The rodeo doc said it's probably best that I get checked out."

"How in the world did you get there?" she asked.

"Well," I said, "it's an interesting story."

UNPLANNED ARRIVAL

The youngest child of hard-working, middle-aged, middle-class, Christian parents and the result of an unplanned pregnancy, my arrival was welcomed with much excitement on May 31, 1977.

My parents already had two sons, one 12 and the other seven, but they remained steadfast that, while unplanned, I was not unloved.

I concur.

My brothers, Jeff and Jay, affectionately referred to me as "the golden child," reaping the proverbial benefits of relaxed parenting. Our opinions contradict.

Jay defined me as funny, odd, perplexing, and slightly annoying with my hint of overconfidence. Jeff viewed me as determined, persistent, and a hair too daring. On some occasions, I was a chameleon, displaying all these traits at the same time.

Specifically, I remember the first Sparks Brothers "Free-for-all Brawl." The three of us engaged in an all-out relentless fight. We turned over furniture and ultimately wrecked Jeff's bedroom.

Jeff was approaching 19, Jay 14, and I was seven. Age was simply a number that day. It was the beginning of a long trend in which I would demonstrate my thrill for jumping in over my head just to see if I could survive.

While I depended on sheer determination, our parents depended on God. Raising three wild boys exceeded their skill set. Without God's influence in our lives, Mom and Dad thought it was possible that we could become whiskey-bent and hell-bound.

Especially me—the mischievous one.

Dad was a deacon at the church, and Momma played the piano. We were at church every time the doors were open. But they didn't push religion on us. They simply lived their faith. Their relationship with Jesus was humble and genuine, and we witnessed their daily obedience to the Lord. They weren't Bible-thumpers, and they never came across as preachy. Mom and Dad just made it known we couldn't ride their coattails into heaven. We each needed our own faith.

Before moving to Fountain Hill, we lived in Marvell, another rural, Delta town in Arkansas. It was there I first felt my own sense of conviction. In March 1989, just a couple of months before my 12th birthday, the Marvell First Baptist Church held a weeklong revival. Like every Sunday, the Sparks family sat on the third row for every service.

I literally broke into a sweat at the conclusion of each service that week. When our preacher made the invitation for anyone who wanted to profess Jesus as Lord to come forward, my stomach moved to my throat. I refused to surrender to the conviction. I simply didn't have the courage to step out in faith.

On the morning of the final day of the revival, I went to school just like every day before. But something was different. A stronger and more powerful conviction came over me. I ignored it as long as I could. Then, as I sat quietly in my reading class, I surrendered to Jesus. I asked for forgiveness and accepted Him as the true Son of God.

When the 6 p.m. service rolled around, I knew I had to follow through during the invitation. So I eased my way out to the aisle, took the preachers hand, and publicly professed my decision to follow Jesus.

I prayed I would live in accordance to God's will, but I had no idea what the Lord's plans were for me. As a new believer in Jesus, I took great comfort in knowing God was in control.

My faith in Christ became the foundation of my story.

Two years later, God revealed to me the first glimpse of His plan. It wasn't as if I thought I needed to do something for God. It was more an idea that God could use me for His purpose.

To be a vessel for God.

Being a vessel for Christ wasn't a new concept. Nor was I unique for feeling this way. In fact, what I felt was an elementary principle of the Christian faith.

Simply put, a container is a container. Whether it holds water, money, or food, it does not become its contents. The container always remains the container. In the same way, life is a container—a vessel that can be used to carry God's purpose on earth (Romans 9).

This idea of making myself a vessel for God started as a feeling, but soon it manifested into a God-given vision.

Slumped over the tiny study in my bedroom, sitting on a small, wooden chair, I humbly asked God for direction in my life.

What followed is hard to explain.

I didn't see heaven. I didn't see Jesus. Yet the vision was powerful, and the experience was life changing.

Before saying "Amen" to conclude the prayer, I felt the presence of God upon me. A quiet calmness fell around me. Everything stood still. With my eyes closed and arms extended, tears fell down my cheeks.

It wasn't scary. Quite the opposite, actually. It was comforting and peaceful. Being surrounded by the power of the Holy Spirit was awe-inspiring.

The vision was clear.

As the scenes unfolded, I saw a glimpse of my future. I was a rodeo bullfighter, performing on grand stages and traveling the world. God was using me to reach audiences that may not otherwise hear of the salvation offered through Christ or see firsthand the joy that is in the lives of those called to His purpose.

Then I heard the voice of God speak to my soul, revealing the purpose for my life. As clear as day, I heard these words loud and clear: "You will go out to witness, encourage, serve, and testify."

I was to glorify God. My light needed to shine so that others might see God's awesomeness.

Matthew 5:16 declares that the purpose for everyone is to: "Let your light shine before others, so that they may see your good works and give glory to your Father who is in heaven." (ESV)

As the vision concluded, I understood the *why*, but the *how* didn't come so easily.

A rodeo bullfighter? I thought. *How is that going to happen?*

CRUCES RODEO

My mom's brothers, John Allen Cruce and Jerry Cruce, owned a small rodeo company in our hometown of Fountain Hill, Arkansas. C&C Rodeo, or "Cruces" as it was commonly referred to, sat just north of our little 150-person community.

Uncle Jerry was a respected bull rider in Arkansas and across the South in his day. In 1976, in fact, he was the Arkansas state champion.

Uncle John Allen rarely competed in rodeo, but he was a respected horse trainer and an even better storyteller.

Two of my aunts, Aunt Dian Ricks (my momma's sister) and Aunt Sharon (Uncle Jerry's wife), were the rodeo's secretaries. My three first cousins were all-around cowboys and helped out around the place. My Uncle John Ricks ran the concession stand.

It was a family business, to say the least.

My grandma, or "Mammaw" as everyone knew her, was the rodeo's biggest fan and my transportation to Cruces.

In rural Arkansas, rodeo was our "Friday Night Lights." No other sport came close. People loved our little rodeo, and hundreds of spectators piled in every weekend from March through October.

When the live action unfolded, fans, family, and instigators flocked to my Uncle John Allen. Everyone knew that when his Bud Light started talking, a scene was sure to follow. From runaway horses to bulls leaping the arena fence, he loved it all. The wilder the better. That's when he would typically proclaim, "John Cruce is on the loose!"

If work needed to be done around Cruces, and you were of blood kin, a job was in your immediate future. And, as typical of many family businesses, we mostly were paid in love, not cash.

One August in 1990, when I was only 13, a cousin and I had

the bright idea to tempt fate in pursuit of a quick dollar. We signed up to compete in the rodeo's most dangerous event—bull riding.

If we aren't going to get rich for pitching in, we thought, *we should at least ride for the jackpot.*

In bull riding, a willing and able human being tries to ride a bull for eight seconds, hanging on with one hand wedged in a rope. The bull's job is to buck, spin, and implode like a balloon that has suddenly released its air.

Sounded easy enough.

I was entered, and thereafter climbed on the back of a bull branded C86. He was a novice bull, but he was plenty fierce for me!

Uncle Jerry gave his fearless nephew a few parting words of wisdom.

"Keep your hand shut, stay up on your rope, and have fun!" he said.

Uncle John Allen then yelled, "Turn 'em out in the big pen, boys!"

And with that, the show was on.

Riding that first bull felt like being in the middle of a tornado! Adrenaline raged through every vein.

But I took Uncle Jerry's advice as literal and didn't open my hand when the ride was over. As a result, my hand remained hung in the bull rope. I was drug around the arena and stepped on every time C86 hoofs crashed down on the dirt.

Uncle Jerry rushed to my rescue, freeing my hand from the rope. It was a sweet relief to my punished body.

I didn't earn a dime. In fact, I didn't even last the required eight seconds to qualify for the jackpot.

But like fighting with my older brothers, the experience was exhilarating.

As I brushed the dirt off and checked out my torn clothes, I thought, *I can't wait to do this again!*

Driving home, Mammaw tried to focus on keeping her old Ford in the middle of Midway Route, not on my battered body.

"Mammaw, what do you think Mom and Dad are going to say?" I asked, breaking the awkward silence.

"I don't know. What do *you* think?" she replied as her eyes sparkled behind her rose-tinted glasses. She didn't have to say anything else. I knew it wasn't going to be good.

As we both expected, my parents didn't take kindly to their baby's condition.

When they saw my clothes were torn beyond repair, my mom frantically asked, "What in the world happened to you?"

How could I rationalize that all was well when I looked like a rag doll? There was no need for me to even try and explain.

"John Allen and Jerry put him on a bull," Mammaw said.

And the parental fireworks show began!

"You've got to be kidding me!" Momma cried.

"Son, didn't you know better?" Dad added.

It was a verbal ping-pong match, and I was the ball. Mammaw was the hypothetical net. When Mom and Dad paused to regroup, she would chime in.

Mammaw caught the rodeo fever years back and was a lifelong fan.

"Claudie," she said to my mom, "there isn't one thing wrong with Jeremy trying his hand at bull riding; boys will be boys!"

My parents begged to differ.

MEETING MY MENTOR

*Why would God call me to reach people through rode*o? I wondered two months later when I received my vision.

I was terrible, inexperienced, and my parents didn't approve.

Knowing how my parents had taken the news of my bull riding experiment, I was reluctant to inform them of my vision. Even though it was a real experience, it felt safer keeping it to myself.

So, for a while, that's what I did.

On March 20, 1991, I went along for a rodeo road trip to Texarkana, Arkansas with Mark and Kim Bowden. Mark is a second cousin. Kim helped my aunts keep the books at my uncles' rodeo. Their two kids and I enjoyed living the rural life together in L.A.—Lower Arkansas. With every weekend that passed, Kim saw my craving for rodeo grow.

I was beyond excited to tag along.

Texarkana hosts an annual bucking bull sale each March. Stock contractors and spectators come to watch the next generation of bucking bulls perform.

We were no different.

I wanted to watch the live action. Mark was intrigued by the bucking bulls, always bragging on the top selling bull. Kim and their kids enjoyed the rodeo atmosphere and fellowship.

While taking in the action, Kim noticed a local celebrity in the stands—Donny Sparks, a champion professional bullfighter.

Kim called to Donny as she pointed at me.

"This boy is a Sparks," she said.

Immediately, Donny fired back as genuine as the day is long.

"Oh, really," he said. "We've gotta be kin."

He made his way to our seats and started to inquire.

From our initial conversation, we gathered that we probably were distant cousins. Perhaps we are, but that day was the start of a friendship that became even closer than kinship.

From my perspective, Donny Sparks could have walked on water. We just didn't have any water for him to prove it!

At the ripe age of 26, he was already a two-time reserve world champion bullfighter in the Professional Rodeo Cowboys Association (PRCA) on the Wrangler Bullfighting Tour. His signature move was to run straight at a raging bull and leap over it from head to tail. It's as if he was competing in a sprint hurdle race—but these hurdles wanted to gore him to death.

By all accounts, he is the greatest and most graceful bull jumper that rodeo has ever seen.

After spending a few hours with Donny on that cold March day, it felt like a safe place to share my vision. Donny didn't question my authenticity, or my naivety—he listened and encouraged. As our conversation continued, the notion of being a rodeo cowboy somehow seemed sensible.

While I was confident that my vision was God-inspired, it was comforting to see someone in the flesh living that exact life.

I believe God sent Donny to me that day to confirm a specific piece of my life's puzzle.

God called me to be a vessel. That was my *why*. My purpose—bullfighting—was to be my *how*.

I left Texarkana sold on fulfilling my God-given dream—no matter the price and no matter the sacrifice!

You can imagine the looks I received when I returned home and finally started sharing my vision.

In some form or fashion, this is what I typically heard: "Say what?" "God said you were going to be a rodeo bullfighter?" "Are you serious?" "You're too small."

Mom and Dad said, "You're dreaming, alright. You are too young, and you *will* get hurt!"

My family always thought I would be a tennis player. Tennis, a sport I'd taken to before we moved to Fountain Hill, was my first love, and I was pretty good at it for my age. There was just one problem: Fountain Hill didn't have any courts. Needless to say, the lack of opportunity to play consistently stalled my progression.

My parents, of course, were quick to see the danger associated with the compound word *bullfighter*.

Understandably so.

A bullfighter is exactly what it sounds like—someone who fights a bull. It is a game of inches. There are no referees. There are no timeouts, and the bull always has home-field advantage. The animal outweighs the fighter 10:1 and is in better physical shape.

The fighter's only edge is his mind.

It requires confidence and nerves of steel.

On the flip side, it takes great humility knowing that the animal can kill you. The fighter's ultimate source of protection comes from God above.

The word *bullfighter* often conjures up images of a Spanish-style *matador de toros*, complete with a red cape. These are the fighters who inspired Ernest Hemingway to write *Death in the Afternoon*, a non-fiction book about the sport.

Bullfighters in rodeo, however, play one of two roles—they are a cowboy protector and/or an American freestyle bullfighter.

As a cowboy protector, the bullfighter serves as a lifesaver during the world's most dangerous sport on dirt, bull riding. The rider's primary goal is to ride the bull for eight seconds. His secondary goal is to return to safety after the ride is complete or after he's thrown to the ground.

A cowboy protector distracts the bull, allowing the rider to safely escape. Uncle Jerry fulfilled this role the day he freed my hand from ol' C86 as I was being dragged around and stepped on.

As the bull rider is making his escape, the bullfighter tries to make himself an easier target. If someone has to take a hit, it is the bullfighter's honor. Yes, literally take a hit from an up to 2,000-pound bull, even if that means being gored, hooked, thrown, stepped on, or worse.

I liken it to the role of the secret service. The difference is that we are smart enough not to get into politics! But it's similar to the way secret service members would literally take a bullet for the person who is in their care. No questions asked, just fulfilling the duties of the office!

The second role of a bullfighter is in freestyle bullfighting, and that's what I was doing in 2000 in Lawton, Oklahoma.

Freestyle is done for the crowd's entertainment or in a competition where bullfighters battle a fighting bull in a one-on-one, man-versus-beast type duel. This is similar to the bullfights popular in the Spanish and Portuguese cultures that captured Hemmingway's imagination.

There are two distinct differences. First, American bulls are not fought to their death. And, second, American bullfighters do not use a red cape to distract the raging bull (who, by the way, is color blind).

The rules are simple. A fighter has 70 seconds to outsmart, trick, dance, fake, jump, and exemplify unbridled courage and determination. When accomplished by an experienced bullfighter, it is poetry in motion, a graceful art.

On the other hand, it can be a complete and catastrophic disaster—the longest 70 seconds of a fighter's life—a true game of survival. It's an endurance test for the mind and body.

Freestyle was Donny's forte.

I longed to practice and mimic his every move.

Using an old 55-gallon metal drum, I engineered a clown barrel and started jumping over invisible bulls. A clown barrel is often used as a prop for a variety of tricks and daring moves, adding a little flare and danger to the performance. For hours upon hours, days upon days, I jumped over countless fanciful bulls.

I would envision a raging bull head-butting the barrel. Taking off from 30 feet back to get a running start, I'd lunge onto the barrel's side, touching down with my left foot, and pushing off the platform as I catapulted up and over the imaginary bull!

In time, Mom and Dad slowly started to understand that my dream was bigger than me. They heard how much I talked and prayed about my future. They saw how much time and energy I put into training.

Being a bullfighter captivated me. Every second was filled with thoughts of fighting bulls. It even replaced my love of tennis, especially as those opportunities continued to dwindle.

I was especially drawn to the athleticism required in freestyle bullfighting. The agility I had learned in tennis was essentially the same footwork—quick pivots, short bursts of speed, and tight turns. Outmaneuvering an angry beast and knowing that the challenge was literally life and death piqued my sense of adventure.

To survive took the application of talent and hard work, but ultimately it was a testament of God's protection.

Now I had a vision, a plan, and a path. But I had no way of knowing the obstacles, forks, or winding roads to come. God's hand was with me. He directed my every step as my aspirations and talents aligned to glorify the Father.

COWBOY LOGIC

1. How are you glorifying God in your current station in life?

2. Have you felt a calling on your life?

3. If so, how are you pursuing it? If not, are you willing to pray that God would reveal His plans for your life?

4. What steps are you taking to prepare for your God-given dream?

In the same way, let your light shine before others, so that they may see your good works and give glory to your Father who is in heaven.

Matthew 5:16 (ESV)

chapter 2
ENCOURAGING WORDS

Principle No. 1: Lend a Hand—Exhortation can Change a Life

I started my freshman year of high school in the fall of 1991. Fountain Hill's enrollment, however, was so small that kindergarten through 12th grade was all under one roof. Transitioning to high school wasn't much of a change.

The only real difference was being eligible to play high school sports. We didn't have enough students to field a football team, so "sports" meant Wildcat basketball and baseball. Basketball had never been a real passion, and my desire to play baseball was fleeting. But the teams needed me, so I played.

Of course, rodeo was my love, and I was determined to find a way to perform. Even though I had jumped a million imaginary bulls and practiced agility drills for countless hours, I needed to get in the arena with real bulls.

C&C Rodeo was the perfect venue to test the waters.

Much to my parents' dismay, and without their full consent, my Mammaw continued to take me to the rodeo and remained my strongest ally.

Uncle Jerry was on hand every weekend and started helping me with the fundamentals. More importantly, he came to my rescue when the bulls overpowered me or when I was struggling with the fears that inevitably set in for a novice stepping into the arena.

As the chute gate swung open to start the rodeo action one

night, for instance, the first bull rider out was immediately thrown. When his back hit the cold, hard ground, a big "thump" rang out.

It was my opportunity to save the day.

As he lay stunned, however, I briefly froze in place. My hesitation prevented me from reaching the scene of the crash fast enough to protect him. The mistake allowed the bull to hook the poor fellow. He was hit in the butt and flung through the air, all while I stood stuck in my tracks.

Bullfighting is arguably the most dangerous role in rodeo. Yet bull riding is often referred to as the "toughest sport on dirt." A bull rider, however, only faces one to three bulls a night. At most, that's a total of 24 seconds, eight seconds at a time!

A bullfighter faces *every* bull and protects *every* rider at the event. The job is not over until the last rider finds safety. So, a bullfighter commonly faces at least 15 bulls each performance, and sometimes as many as 60.

As a kid, I lacked nearly all of the physical traits that make a great bullfighter. A 15-year-old weighing a buck 30 and standing 6 feet tall doesn't scream physical prowess. I imagine the ideal bullfighter is around 5-foot-10 and weighs 180-190 pounds. He is solid enough to take the physical pounding, yet agile enough to outmaneuver a charging bull.

While tennis, basketball, and baseball had provided a solid foundation of agility, bullfighting was my first exposure to contact sports. Win, lose, or draw, a bullfighter must distract the bull's attention off of the fallen rider and onto himself. This often results in being hooked and tossed around; hence the contact sports reference.

Mom and Dad couldn't fathom how their skinny baby boy could possibly compete with a 1,800-pound bull. But every Friday and Saturday night, I'd throw my gear bag in Mammaw's old Ford truck, and she'd spin the tires on our gravel driveway as we headed north.

Her truck was a *three on the tree* (a manual transmission with the gear shift on the steering wheel column), and my 81-year-old Mammaw drove it like she stole it.

Her knees were bad, so pushing the clutch was a challenge, but she made it work. It was a small price to pay for her freedom. As she sped down back roads, Mammaw would pull herself up holding tight to the steering wheel, gaining leverage to push the clutch and shift gears.

I teased her every time.

"Grind 'em till you find 'em, Mammaw," I'd say.

Pulling onto the rodeo grounds always brought sweet relief. Just knowing we survived the ride was awesome. But it also meant I was moments away from trying the moves I had practiced. Realistically, I wasn't about to jump a bull. I would simply get to test my agility if a bull charged.

Roughly two months into my trial period, I got my first chance to free a rider's hand as he was being dragged. In rodeo terms, it's called "working a hang up." The goal is to keep the bull from trampling the rider while also helping free the rider's entangled hand from the bull rope.

As I moved into position, the bull's right front hoof came crashing down on my left leg just above my ankle. It hurt a little, but the pain wasn't overwhelming. Adrenaline and the thrill of being able to help the cowboy minimized the discomfort.

The rider escaped and I limped away.

As I caught my breath, I mumbled to Uncle Jerry, "My leg is hurt."

I'm not sure exactly what he said, but it was something to the effect that I should *suck it up!*

There were more bull riders to protect. They would have been fine without me, but it was my job to protect them. Playing in pain was part of the job description for a bullfighter, so I stayed in the arena to fulfill my duties.

When the last bull rider had found safety, I limped over to Mammaw and complained about my bummed leg.

We loaded up and spun gravel en route to Uncle Jerry and Aunt Sharon's house. They lived less than a mile away, and Mammaw needed the closest phone to call my parents. She didn't necessarily need to whisk me away to medical attention; she just enjoyed taking advantage of the opportunity to speed!

I limped inside and propped my leg up as Mammaw rang my parents.

"Claudie, Jeremy says his leg is hurt," she said. I was okay, she told my mom, I'd just "been stepped on and was complaining about my leg hurting."

Mom didn't like what she heard, so she and Dad drove over to see my injury firsthand. When they arrived, it was clear they weren't happy, and Mom insisted that we go to the ER. Sure enough, X-rays revealed a fractured left leg.

A broken bone wouldn't deter me, though. Just like staying in the arena after the incident, this, too, was part of the game.

Ernest Hemingway wrote that, "Bullfighting is the only art in which the artist is in danger of death and in which the degree of brilliance in the performance is left to the fighter's honor." While his reference is to traditional matadors, the risks and dangers are just the same.

My minor injury was merely a small price to pay for honor. The doctor who cast my leg suggested I would be out of action for six weeks. *Four weeks max*, I decided.

Some of my classmates said, "I told you that you were too small." Others continued to say I was too tall and too fragile.

I quickly realized that a big heart would have to compensate for a skinny body. Coming back to the arena in four weeks versus six was my first statement.

GO TO 'EM, SON

By the time the season ended in October, I had earned the nickname, "Wormy, the Rodeo Clown." Wormy was a pretty accurate description of my physical stature. I was a long, skinny kid!

The Bible is full of examples of God providing for those who are disadvantaged. David is one of my favorites. He was still a kid the day he was taking provisions to his brothers in King Saul's army. That's when he heard Goliath's challenge. All of the other soldiers backed down, but David stood up. Never once did his physical limitations deter him from pursuing his God-given assignment of defeating the Philistine. It mattered very little to David what people thought of his small stature and lofty ambition.

Likewise, the size disadvantage and mounting odds never entered my mind.

My family thought my passion would fade, or that I would be killed in the process. But the feedback I received, though often well intended, was simply background noise compared to the loud and clear calling I had already received. When God speaks and calls you to a task, how *other* people view you or your mission should be irrelevant.

Have you ever noticed that people who are paralyzed by fear in their own life try to share their gift of negativity? Or maybe you've experienced the type of person who is fine with you chasing your endeavor as long as it isn't bigger than their dream. Unfortunately, we all encounter a few of these toxic personalities. My least favorite among them is the person who simply wants to see others fail.

How sad.

In a twisted way, they believe their "success" is only attained through the failure of others.

A mind-over-matter attitude quickly became my primary tool to combat negativity and to overcome physical limitations.

Yes, people initially invested in my aspirations, but I got started with the help of a very small inner circle.

It was in my youth that I learned the importance of Principle No. 1: Lend a Hand. It's a simple cowboy code—a hand up, not a hand out. To me, the Lend a Hand principle suggests that exhortation can change a life.

Donny Sparks consistently modeled this principle. Knowing its impact on my life, I adopted the principle to help guide me throughout my journey.

Few people poured into my life at the start of my bullfighting career like Donny. It forever changed me. How I serve others—inside and outside of the rodeo arena—is a direct reflection of his example.

Donny didn't fill my head with hot air or make me believe I was a bullfighting protégé. He simply encouraged me. In turn, his encouragement helped build my confidence.

Uncle John Allen also took an interest in my passion for bullfighting. He could be a tough man to please, but as I improved and he saw my commitment, he supported my efforts. It was a big deal for me when he called my dad to express his confidence in my development.

On the other hand, he didn't always know how to express that confidence or support when he was with me. In fact, I often got the feeling I was in the way. More than once I'd seen him grin ear to ear when a bull hooked me to the ground.

The C&C Rodeo Company was the biggest show in town. He had tickets to sell, and kinship was equated to cheap labor. I was his free bullfighter, risking life and limb to learn the craft while thrilling spectators by being hooked, gored, and stepped on for their viewing pleasure.

At that time, I had no idea about the personal demons he battled. All I knew was that it often seemed as if my "hookings" brought a smile to his face.

Most Saturday mornings, John Allen would go to the livestock sale in neighboring Warren, Arkansas to buy and sell cattle. What brought him the greatest joy, however, was finding mean bulls for the rodeo. He typically called me after the sale to remind me to bring my bullfighting gear to the rodeo. My gear was a hand-me-down football girdle and an old pair of black Nike cleats. And the bulls never had a problem finding the chinks in my light armor.

On Saturday nights, John Allen expected me to fight the new bull in a brief one-on-one match after the rider found safety. It was as if I were one of Hemingway's matadors, and John Allen was a stately official observing the action. In the name of entertainment, I would try to survive a raging mad bull until he'd seen enough action or until I surrendered.

Brilliance and honor were typically trumped by escape and evasion. Survival was about all that I could manage.

From a safe distance away, John Allen would yell, "Go to him, son!" If you heard him, however, you'd know it wasn't an encouraging voice from the grandstands. He spoke in a sarcastic tone that made me feel like his greatest thrill was generated from my failure. Regardless, I knew he enjoyed selling tickets.

I grew to despise the phrase, "Go to him, son."

Every Saturday afternoon before Mammaw would pick me for the rodeo, I'd call Donny. It didn't matter if Donny was traveling, performing, or resting, he always welcomed my calls. Sometimes it took all of my courage to simply describe the latest sale barn bull John Allen had bought. It was a given; the bull was big, mean, and had horns like daggers, which John Allen affectionately called "clown stabbers."

Over the phone, Donny reiterated the bullfighting fundamentals. "Stick to the basics," he would say. "Make a tight circle, drive to the bull's shoulder, step toward his flank, and go around and around." He was confident my chances of survival increased when keeping it simple.

Donny even put a positive twist on the phrase that I disliked the most.

"When your uncle says, 'Go to him, son,' take the fight to the bull," Donny said. "Become the aggressor and leave him with something to talk about. You can do it."

Honestly, I didn't have the foggiest idea what I was doing inside the arena. However, I knew that at least one person believed in me and one person protected me. God and encouraging words helped me survive my fair share of mean sale barn bulls.

As time passed, my love for rodeo and bullfighting continued to grow. More and more people started to pour into me.

Uncle Jerry gave me my first cowboy hat, a white Bailey Hat Company straw hat with a light blue cross on the side. I recall that moment as if it were yesterday. It was actually a hat that someone left behind at the rodeo. He had put it in the lost-and-found closet, but no one had claimed it.

Uncle Jerry and Aunt Sharon thought if I was going to be a bullfighter, I needed my own hat. Loyd Ketchum was a world champion bullfighter sponsored by Bailey Hats, and for me to have a hat like his was better than any cash payment for working at the rodeo!

My oldest brother, Jeff, became my biggest fan and supported my every need. He paid to upgrade my gear, spending $400 alone on a customized vest that protected my chest and back.

My parents decided that as determined as I was, I'd continue finding ways to pursue my calling. Not only did they start to embrace my passion, they soon stopped questioning Mammaw after every rodeo. Mom and Dad transformed from worried parents into great prayer warriors interceding on my behalf. Safety and protection were their continuous prayer.

My brother Jay was also an advocate. He wanted to see me succeed. Despite being away in college, he always called to hear my rodeo tales.

Long before I showed an ounce of potential, a whole slew of people took turns hauling me to rodeos across the southland. I provided the comic relief, and they provided the wisdom, knowledge, and all-important transportation when Mammaw couldn't take me.

One Friday afternoon, the high school's secretary paged me over the intercom: "Jeremy Sparks to the principal's office, Jeremy to the principal's office."

What in the world could I have done?

I hustled to the office thinking that my dad needed to see me. Not this time. Turned out, I had a visitor.

"Sparks, what are you doing?"

It was bullfighter Art McDaniel.

"I'm in class," I said. "What are you doing, Art?"

"I'm headed to Malvern to the rodeo," he said. "Do you want to come?"

That was like asking a bull if it wants to take a turn inside a china shop. I was always ready to tear down the rodeo trail.

"Yes!" I said with great excitement.

I rushed to inform Dad, who was also the school's principal, that Art had invited me to the rodeo.

"Dad, can I please miss the remainder of the school day?" I begged.

Dad agreed.

Shortly thereafter, off to Malvern we went.

Just as we were leaving the school, Art asked if I was hungry. I was skinny, but that didn't mean I couldn't down some food.

"Man, you know I'm always hungry," I said as we both laughed.

He whipped his old car in at the local market and inside the store we scurried. On the endcap of a produce isle, fresh bananas were stacked to the ceiling.

"Do you like bananas, Sparks?" Art asked.

"Yea, I like bananas."

Art bagged up several bunches of the bananas and proceeded to check out.

Five miles down the road, Art piped up.

"Well, Sparks, you aren't eating those bananas I bought?"

He grabbed my head and attempted to put me in a headlock while cruising 75 miles per hour. Art was built like an armored tank. I knew how this was about to play out.

Real quick-like, I started to peel and eat a couple of bananas. Anything to avoid his big brother treatment.

After finishing the first couple of bananas, he puffed his chest out and said, "You have two more bunches to eat!"

He was serious.

For the next two hours, I crammed bananas down my throat. The banana exercise was just one more lesson in mental toughness. My love for bananas, the smell of bananas, and all things banana died on the road to Malvern.

"I'm not eating any more dang bananas," I told Art, "but I'm not missing any road trips, either!"

When the Arkansas State Fair and Rodeo came to Little Rock, a family from our community invited me to tag along. As a cowboy drifter in training, I politely accepted the invitation.

Maybe, just maybe, I can catch a glimpse of the bull riding and meet the bullfighters.

Soon after arriving in Little Rock, I finagled my way to the arena where the workers were setting up for the rodeo. Tractor drivers were plowing the dirt. Technical folks were testing the sound system. It was a beautiful sight.

To my far right, about 100 yards away, I caught a glance of the three bullfighters. Panic set in. I wasn't expecting to lay eyes on anyone so soon. But there they stood: World Champion Rick Chatman, National Finals Rodeo Bullfighter and Barrelman Leon Coffee, and the ever-popular Jeff Grigsby.

I recognized them from articles and photos I'd seen in the *Pro-Rodeo Sports News*. While we only had one television channel in Fountain Hill, we did have a post office. Twice a month, my subscription of the PSN magically appeared. For me, each issue offered a window into my future.

Seeing these three guys in person was pure bliss.

Nothing was going to keep me from introducing myself. Not even a panic attack!

I walked straight toward Rick, stuck out my hand, and said, "I'm Jeremy Sparks."

My name was all that came to mind, so I said it with confidence and excitement.

"Jeremy, nice to meet you," Rick replied.

He introduced me to Leon and Jeff, and we talked for an hour. As they prepared their clown barrel and props for the night's rodeo, I watched intently. To say the least, I was inclined to share my dream with them.

All three were supportive and listened closely.

They were living that very dream!

Jeff took a white bandana from his bullfighting outfit and handed it to me.

"If you're going to be a bullfighter, you need a bandana," he said.

Printed on the bandana was "Wrangler Bullfighting" with a

picture of the world's most notorious fighting bull, Crooked Nose. These were exclusive for the fighters on the acclaimed Wrangler Bullfighting Tour.

It was a priceless gift. Clearly a kind gesture that motivated me to keep on keeping on. My feet never touched the ground as I walked back to the stock show!

As my high school years progressed, my bullfighting skills continued to slowly develop. Donny never missed an opportunity to encourage me. Art never missed an opportunity to haze me. And I never missed a rodeo road trip.

My senior year, Donny invited me to the ProRodeo in Texarkana, Arkansas to experience firsthand the thrill of professional rodeo. While I'd enjoyed palling around with Art at amateur rodeos, being with Donny at ProRodeo's was always on another level.

He and his twin brother, Ronny, made up Double Trouble. They were two of the most talented bullfighters in America. Each year, it was a dogfight to see which twin would prevail as the world champion.

Sitting courtside, the duo continually inspired me in the beauty of bullfighting. Just as I watched Rick and his crew in Little Rock, I was glued to Donny and Ronny's every move.

When the rodeo ended, they did a meet-and-greet for the fans and spectators. Double Trouble made sure every person in the autograph line received a warm welcome and individual attention.

Donny and Ronny were as genuine with the first kid as they were with the last adult. It was the same authenticity Donny extended to me at the Texarkana bull sales four years prior. They made eye contact, asked each person his name, and made random small talk.

After easily spending two hours meeting and greeting (while his wife and young son waited patiently), Donny said, "Jeremy, when you make it to the level where people want to talk to you solely based on what you do, make time for them."

Donny didn't say, *if* you make it to the level, he said *when* you make it.

Those words made a powerful impact on me.

I thought to myself—*Donny Sparks, the best bullfighter ever— just said, "when" you make it.*

It was October 1994.

While learning the bullfighting fundamentals was necessary, exhortation was essential to my development. People lending me a hand changed my life.

We may not understand each other's journey, but we can encourage one another along the way. In Romans 12, Paul talks about service in the Body of Christ.

"We have different gifts, according to the grace given to each of us. If your gift is prophesying, then prophesy in accordance with your faith; if it is serving, then serve, if it is teaching, then teach; if it is to encourage, then give encouragement..." (Romans 12:6-8, NIV)

Some of the most rewarding events in my life occurred when offering hope and encouragement to others. The *Lend a Hand* principle can be applied by anyone, at any time.

For instance, one of my best memories is from my senior year when God used me to share the Gospel with my good friend and fellow cowboy, Matt Williams. We were at the Arkansas High School Rodeo State Finals, and he was on the verge of winning his first state title in the tie-down roping event.

We stayed up all night practicing and talking about chasing our cowboy dreams. As time wore on, I felt led to share the Gospel with him.

"Matt, I know that you are one day away from being crowned

the state champion," I said, "but do you know that even that is not enough for eternity?"

I explained how God loved us so much that He sent his Son Jesus to die for our sins, so that through faith alone we may have eternal life. He accepted God's grace in that moment.

It was awesome to know that God used me, among others, to change the trajectory of Matt's life forever.

Lending a hand is a simple choice that can make a huge impact.

Uncle Jerry made a simple choice when he taught me the fundamentals and when he gave me a prized cowboy hat.

Donny made a simple choice to walk over and talk to me one day in Texarkana, to talk to me almost weekly about the art of bullfighting, and to use phrases like "when you make it."

Art made a simple choice to take me with him to the rodeo in Malvern (and stuff me with bananas along the way).

Rick Chatman, Leon Coffee, and Jeff Grigsby made a simple choice to listen and encourage a stranger while they prepared for a rodeo in Little Rock.

I made a simple choice to say what God had put on my heart in my conversation with Matt.

What simple choices can you make today to lend a hand?

COWBOY LOGIC

1. Who are you currently encouraging to aim high?

2. What are additional ways you can support others in their journey?

3. How has encouraging others in turn blessed you?

Let us consider how we may spur one another on toward love and good deeds; encouraging one another.

Hebrews 10:24 (NIV)

chapter 3

IN A FLASH

Principle No. 2: Step Through—Faith Makes All Things Possible

In 1995, just weeks before high school graduation, I was offered a rodeo scholarship by McNeese State University in Lake Charles, Louisiana.

This was huge for me. I had good grades, so I knew I could go to college. But I was by no means as polished as many other cowboys in our area, so the chance to compete in college rodeos was exciting news.

While freestyle bullfighting wasn't an event in the collegiate ranks, there was a recurring need for cowboy protection bullfighters.

McNeese held weekly practice sessions and took part in 10 regional collegiate rodeos each school year. It was a great opportunity to continue learning the craft and to take the next big step in my journey, so I accepted the offer.

As stated earlier, my dad was my school principal, and my mom taught social studies for grades 7-12. So they stressed the importance of higher education. We had made a pact early on that I would earn a college degree. Fearing injuries, they didn't want my future limited to just rodeo. They wanted me to have something to fall back on.

I promised my folks I would earn a degree, so getting one where I could keep refining my rodeo skills sounded like a win-win.

Coach Smith, or "Mr. John" as I preferred to call him, knew about my overall cowboy skills. They were average at best, but he thought I would grow and become competitive in the roping events. He also figured I would stay academically eligible to compete on the team. Just like all collegiate sports, rodeo's student-athletes had to maintain a 2.0 grade point average while enrolled in at least 12-credit hours.

Mr. John and I discussed my passion for rodeo. We talked at length about my desire to one day fight bulls on the world's largest stages. He was counting on me to score points in the roping events, something I thought I could do. But I made it clear my focus was mastering the art of bullfighting. Mr. John was on board.

Two Arkansas cowgirls—Becky Collins and Courtney Smith— also were awarded scholarships to McNeese. Like me, they accepted sight unseen.

All we could talk about was becoming big-time rodeo stars. I simply had to survive the three summer months until we could head to McNeese for classes and College Rodeo 101.

My scholarship covered roughly half of the annual tuition and fees. The rest was up to me and my family. Mom and Dad committed to helping financially, and Jeff pledged his continued support. But it was going to take all of us to keep me in college and on the rodeo trail, so picking up a summer job and earning cash was paramount.

My parents used hard work and education to provide a great middle-class life for my brothers and me. I didn't completely understand how much effort it took to invest in our future. But I clearly saw that when determination and opportunity collide, it becomes a game-changer for individuals, families, and even future generations.

Knowing how they'd sacrificed for me, I was determined to pull my weight.

NEARLY DEAD IN THE SHED

Fountain Hill was replete with farmland and pastures. Tomato farms lined most dirt roads, and extra farmhands were always needed for the summer harvest. It wasn't easy work and it wasn't lucrative work. It was simply work. It was just what I needed—a paying job.

Knowing it would help fund my dreams, I was excited to start my job on the Meeks Tomato Farm. Mr. James Meeks owned the farm just southwest of town, roughly 15 minutes from our home. No matter the task, I made myself available. If he needed a driver to haul the day's harvest to the market or a hand to unload the produce for buyers, I consistently volunteered. I wanted to maximize the opportunity, and he was more than willing to put me to work for minimum wage.

The first couple of months couldn't pass fast enough. I worked all week just to rodeo on the weekend. By July it was hard to focus on the farm work; the next phase of life at McNeese was merely weeks away.

On a July day that reached 105 degrees, however, my life was forever changed when I performed the most routine of tasks—I plugged in an industrial shop fan to provide some relief to the heat in the tomato shed.

As I mentioned earlier in this story, the cord had been partly severed and I was standing in water. So, instead of sending a cool breeze through the shed, the cord sent a flash of electricity throughout my skinny body.

The jolt from the 220-volt outlet created just the right amount of current to knock me down, dislodging the power cord from my hand when I hit the ground—a circumstance that possibly saved my life. A little more current could have meant death on contact.

The electricity that went through my chest cavity caused one of my heart valves to become slightly separated. The shock created an atrocious irregular heartbeat. It also caused neuro-inhibitory syncope and dizziness—a condition that would cause me routinely to faint. At any time, in any place, and typically without warning, I would stop, drop, and eye roll.

Given my condition, the doctors recommended that I withdraw from McNeese State before I'd even put a boot on the campus.

My plans shorted out that hot July afternoon.

But God had a plan.

STEPPING THROUGH IN FAITH

Principle No. 2 emerged from this major life event. I call it Step Through, and it's all about embracing faith.

A step through is a signature move in freestyle bullfighting where the fighter fakes one direction and immediately goes the opposite. It deceives the oncoming bull as he charges a moving target. When the bull blows by and narrowly misses the fighter, the fighter pivots and spins 180 degrees to immediately square up with the bull and continue the trick and fancy footwork.

A traditional matador would use a red cape for this trick, but a rodeo bullfighter uses only his body. It takes years to master the step through because it calls for skill, bravery, and unwavering faith.

The Step Through principle teaches that faith makes all things possible. I'm not talking about self-confidence. I'm talking about faith that God will carry you through regardless of the obstacles you face, the sins you commit, or the unexpected changes in your journey.

It was a confusing time. I had no reason to think I was on the wrong path, and the new path sure didn't seem like it would lead me where God had called me to go. *So how would I get there?*

I still trusted God, but I often asked, "Why?" Frankly, it didn't make sense to me. But Proverbs 3:5 calls us to, "Trust in the Lord with all your heart and lean not on your own understanding." (NIV)

Many times in my life, that verse has been easier said than done, easier read than applied. In the days, months, and even years following the accident, there were many times I felt I could navigate my life better than God. But He always found a way to refocus my attention, although thankfully it never again involved 220 volts of electricity.

Since I couldn't accept the scholarship at McNeese State, I enrolled at the University of Central Arkansas (UCA) in the fall of 1995.

UCA had previously offered me its Chancellor's Academic Scholarship. It was never my plan to accept it, but it was a welcomed financial relief. My heart wasn't really into college outside of McNeese, but I wanted to make good on my promise to my parents that I would earn a degree.

UCA was closer to home and closer to Arkansas Children's Hospital in Little Rock, where I remained under the care of their cardiology team. They had prescribed four medications, some that I had to take three times a day, to help mend my heart and reduce the fainting spells. My physical activities were restricted to prevent undue stress on my heart.

Translation: No more rodeo.

I pledged to the Pi Kappa Alpha fraternity and made new friends, but I missed rodeo and my traveling partners.

For no real reason, I majored in biology with the lofty goal of going to medical school. Maybe since I was spending so much time at the hospital, I thought I would become a doctor.

Who knows?!

Every week, I had to visit the university nurse to log my blood pressure. Every month for the next two years, I traveled 30 miles south from Conway to Arkansas Children's Hospital for observation. And every month for two straight years, I heard the same thing: "No change, stay the course, keep taking your medication."

UCA was as far from rodeo as I had ever been. As each day passed, my desire to return exponentially increased. Although my physical activities were restricted, over time I began testing the waters by playing limited tennis and doing light exercises.

Little by little, God started to restore my strength and stamina. I hadn't picked up a tennis racquet in eight years, but hitting the ball came back easier than riding a bicycle. It felt good to reconnect with my first love.

Seeing that my physical endurance had increased, I finally was able to wean off the four medications. This wasn't what the doctors had ordered, but neither was the exercise. My unbridled faith coupled with waning patience outweighed any medical risks.

Watching time pass was no longer an option. For months I'd been attending a small group Bible study led by professor and evangelist, Dr. Travis Plumlee. Every Wednesday night, we met to study the Word and pray. While the majority of the guys were called to pastor, my call was different. As time passed, I felt led to return to my passion and fulfill my dream, not wait, and wait, and wait.

Three months into implementing the self-prescribed plan, I decided to reveal my big secret to my doctors and my parents. Mom and Dad met me at the hospital, as usual. As we walked into the exam room, I was nervous and a little shaky. Yet I knew this was the right time.

My medical condition was unique, so the attending physician typically wanted the residents and fellows to study my case. There were six or seven people packed into the small examination room on this day. It was cold and smelled like plastic packaging materials, like so many hospital rooms smell. I no longer opted for the gowns.

After two years, there wasn't a lot of me that they hadn't already seen.

The doctors took turns listening to my heartbeat and taking my blood pressure—while I was sitting and then standing and then lying down.

The cardiologist asked pointed questions about my stamina and the frequency of my fainting spells.

I thought to myself, *I quit journaling their occurrence when I stopped taking the meds!*

"Stamina is better," I said. "Haven't fainted since the last appointment."

I didn't know the specific reasons for their questions; I just felt it didn't matter.

When everyone was done poking, prodding, listening, and questioning me, the attending physician said those words that I had grown so accustomed to hear.

"No change, stay the course, keep taking your medication."

In a calm, but assertive, voice I announced, "I stopped taking all the medications months ago. I've been working out regularly and playing tennis, so it is great news to learn that you don't see a change!"

By the appearance on some of the faces in the room, it looked like it was their turn to faint!

My parents escorted me out of the room.

"Jeremy," my mom cried, "are you serious?!"

"Mom, you heard the doctors," I said. "I'm fine."

Needless to say, it was uncomfortable facing my parents. They wanted to celebrate the good news, but they exercised caution. They liked the results but were concerned that I had taken matters into my own hands.

The doctor's final discharge note, dated June 2, 1997 read, "Jeremy decided that he might as well stop taking his medication. It is my impression that he is doing well off all medications, so there is no further reason for him to return to the Arrhythmia Clinic."

Two years had passed and with no medical green light in sight, I had to take action. And I was glad I did.

JUST IN TIME

I couldn't see God's plan at the time, but clearly He was at work.

During the time I was sidelined, Uncle Jerry acquired a really mean fighting bull. It was ready for the "bright lights" and "big pens," as Uncle John Allen would say.

JIT, as we called him, was a decent-sized bull, roughly 1,600 pounds. He also was quick and agile, with two intimidating horns. And he would hook, paw, and snort at a strong breeze.

His name stood for Just In Time. And anyone who fought JIT was just in time for a hooking, goring, stomping, or thrashing. Uncle Jerry wanted JIT to have a chance to fight on the prestigious Wrangler Bullfighting Tour.

As God would establish, I was home from UCA visiting Mom and Dad one weekend in early March 1996. Over the same weekend, there was a freestyle bullfighting event in nearby Monroe, Louisiana. The organizers had promised Uncle Jerry that JIT could audition. He simply needed to get JIT to Monroe in time for the show. So he enlisted the help of his son, J.R., and me to haul JIT to the "big pen."

When we unloaded JIT off the trailer, he bolted into the arena. As usual, he tried to hook, paw, and snort at everything that moved.

One local guy mustered the guts to get in the arena with him. It took 4.5 seconds for JIT to knock the wind out of his sails! That was all the time needed for Harper and Morgan Rodeo Company to make us a cash offer—more than $3,000, as I recall. The money wasn't important, it was the opportunity to see JIT make the tour that we valued.

The majority of the world's best bullfighters, along with a few up and comers, were scheduled to perform in Monroe, so J.R. and I were beyond eager to stick around and watch.

In addition to Donny and Ronny, three other World Champions and the young and talented Mike Matt from Cut Bank, Montana were entered in the competition.

Mike was a reserved yet cocky fellow, having recently qualified for his first National Finals—the Super Bowl of professional rodeo.

My relationship with Donny and Ronny got us into the bullfighters' dressing room. We made some small talk, but their focus was preparing for battle.

As Ronny changed into his bullfighting attire, he handed me his belt and buckle.

"Jeremy," he said, "how about you try this on?"

This can't be happening!

I nervously reached out for Ronny's most prized trophy—his 1995 world champion buckle. It was solid gold.

"It's worth $15,000," he said with a grin. "Don't drop it."

As I threaded the belt through the loops of my Wrangler jeans, I couldn't believe I was in the room with gold buckles, much less getting a chance to wear one.

"Make sure you wear it upside down," Donny said.

"Upside down?" I asked.

"Yea, that way when you look down, you can read it!" he joked.

No one wears a buckle upside down, I thought, but I certainly didn't have the nerve to say it. Nevertheless, his point was taken. I couldn't help but constantly marvel at the champ's sparkling prize.

After the event, Mike Matt spotted me talking with Donny.

"Sparks, come here," he yelled in our direction.

I assumed he was calling for Donny since I had only met him a few hours earlier and we both answered to "Sparks."

"Jeremy, I guess he's yelling for you, because I know he's not yelling at me," Donny said.

So off I hustled. Mike basically threw his gear bag in my direction and said, "Carry this!" in a pointed tone.

As is customary with rodeo athletes, calling a loved one after each event was Mike's next obligation. He strutted to the pay phone some 20 yards away. As he called his lady friend, I stood guard over his gear bag as if it had the president's nuclear codes in it! After all, "Wrangler National Finals Bullfight Contestant" was embroidered on it. It was a big deal, and I didn't mind being associated with a winner!

Being back in the rodeo atmosphere was priceless. My motivation meter was pegged out! It was inspiring to see a group of guys who shared a common vision and who simply wanted to live their dreams.

Donny saw how much I loved being in that environment, so he promised that when I turned 21, he would take me to the National Finals Rodeo.

BRIGHT LIGHTS IN SIN CITY

Returning to school wasn't easy. I continued to struggle finding my purpose at UCA. I longed more than ever for the rodeo life. I turned 21 days after the 1998 spring semester ended, and that very evening my phone rang.

"Happy birthday, big boy," Donny said. "Are you ready for Vegas?"

From June to December, I worked odd jobs, saving enough walking change for the trip. There were long days on the Hancock

Farm fixing fences and feeding cattle. Long nights at the Roller-McNutt Funeral Home serving as an apprentice mortician and funeral director. Any free time was spent as a life skills trainer at the human development center helping mentally and physically challenged adults. Pretty much, I was willing to do any job that would finance a trip of a lifetime.

For 10 straight days in early December, the world's best cowboys and cowgirls converge on Las Vegas to contend for a world championship. Back then, there were four rounds of competition for the top six bullfighters on the Wrangler Bullfighting Tour. The champion was awarded a gold buckle just like the one Ronny let me wear.

Donny had competed six times for a shot at the title, and I aspired to one day have my own shot. So the idea of going to the NFR made me happier than a five-year-old spending the night at Chuck E. Cheese!

Final exams at UCA were scheduled the week after the NFR, so it wasn't the ideal time for me to miss classes. My grades already had slipped out of control. The idea of becoming a doctor was driven by all the wrong reasons, so it never provided much motivation. And given the shape of my grades, the chances of me getting into medical school were a million to one.

Medical school may have been a long shot, but I was a shoe-in for our Las Vegas trip. I wasn't going to let a little thing like missing a few classes hold me back.

A slight delay at the Little Rock airport caused me to run late. I almost missed meeting Donny at our connecting flight in Dallas. The pilot recognized Donny when he boarded and graciously held the plane for me. This was just the first time his celebrity benefited me on the trip.

We landed in Vegas that night and the sky was ablaze with the bright city lights. I had never seen anything like it. Fountain Hill didn't even have a stoplight, and now I found myself in the middle of millions of lights, most of them flashing some message to me. It was sensory overload, but I was "entered," as the rodeo cowboys like to say—willing, able, and eager to get the party started!

We couldn't even get to our room at the Gold Coast Hotel and Casino without people wanting to talk to Donny. He usually introduced me the same way: "This is my cousin, Jeremy!" There wasn't a better compliment in my mind.

When he wanted to pull a fast one, he claimed me as a nephew. After all, we were both tall, slender, and shared similar facial features. But when I was overtaken by the bright lights and scenery, he didn't claim that same kinship.

The first night on the town, I bet $1,000 on one hand of blackjack. It was a crazy feeling, but something about it felt right. Strangers were high-fiving me, whooping and hollering, and having a wild cowboy kind of time. When the dealer hit blackjack, however, it didn't feel good at all.

My buzz was killed as I thought about explaining the situation to Donny and living on $500 for the next two weeks. He didn't disown me, but it was awkward. At times, it felt more like being with a stepdad who had Mom on speed dial than it did being with my hero. He wasn't impressed by my "boy meets world" experience.

Mike Matt had qualified for his fourth consecutive Wrangler Bullfight Finals and was the two-time defending world champion. He was favored to three-peat, despite coming off a broken ankle in Memphis earlier in the season.

Mike hadn't changed since I met him in Monroe. He was still quiet, cocky, and, frankly, a little hard to read.

In the first round, he drew the fighting bull of the year. A big, treacherous, white speckled bull with thick horns, appropriately named Spotted Demon. In a marquee matchup, it was the defending world champion versus the fighting bull of the year.

Before the fight was over, Spotted Demon stepped on Mike and reinjured his ankle. Mike was forced to withdraw from the rest of the NFR. It was heartbreaking to witness.

That night, Donny and I took some ice to Mike's room and tried to make small talk. Donny tried to encourage him as only a veteran fighter who has been in those shoes could. His words were well-intended but fell on deaf ears.

When Mike went to bed, Donny drifted back to our room, and I headed out on the town. Vegas in 1998 was by far the wildest experience of my life. I drank too much, stayed out too late, and made far too many bad decisions. Donny used every one of my mistakes as a teaching opportunity. (And he still does!)

His finer points:

- You know these people only want to talk to you because of what we do.

- One of these nights, you are going to wake up in the tub covered in ice and with a sign around your neck saying, "Call 911, we have your kidney!"

- God gave every man two heads, and just enough blood to use one at a time.

- I will call your momma if I need to.

I returned from those 10 days knowing without a doubt that I was quitting college and hitting the rodeo trail. It was a purely selfish motivation, however, not a mindset connected to fulfilling my calling.

Donny pleaded with me to finish my degree. He understood that even those who "make it" would one day need a second career. His guidance and my promise to Mom and Dad were the only two things that kept me in college.

Four exams—organic chemistry, molecular biology, trigonometry, and leadership—stood between me and Christmas break.

Dr. Mike Moran, my biology professor, was notoriously difficult and didn't like excuses. I stopped in his office and tried to plead a case for my documented ignorance on the subject of molecular biology. Seeing that the conversation wasn't going my direction, I dropped a hint that I might be joining the rodeo circuit full time.

As serious as a heart attack I said, "Sir, I'm thinking about quitting school and being a bullfighter."

Without even looking up, he said, "Jeremy, I think that's the best thing you could do; become a rodeo clown." Based on my grades he, too, was dead serious.

The following Wednesday night at Dr. Plumlee's Bible study, I sincerely repented for my poor choices in Vegas and prayed for direction. A crossroad was nearing. Not knowing exactly what to do, I felt led to visit an old friend and rodeo cowboy, Chad Saunders. He lived about 20 minutes north of campus in the rural community of Wooster.

When I arrived at the end of Seldom Rest Ranch Road, Chad was outside practicing for his next rodeo.

"Sparky, what in the world are you doing?" he asked as I made my way in his direction.

"Chadro, I've come to see you," I said. "We need to talk. I think I'm going to transfer colleges and get back into rodeo."

Without missing a beat, he looked me in the eyes and said, "Sparky, I think you should take a leap of faith and do it."

COWBOY LOGIC

1. The Step Through principle teaches that faith makes all the difference. When has faith allowed you to overcome a seemingly overwhelming obstacle?

2. How do you typically respond to setbacks?

3. What challenges are you preparing for that demand the faith referenced in the Step Through principle?

Trust in the LORD with all your heart and lean not on your own understanding.

Proverbs 3:5 (NIV)

chapter 4
PHOENIX RISING

Principle No. 3: Bear Down—The Hard Work of Preparation
Never Ends

By the time grades came out at UCA, I already had started the process of transferring. It was a good thing, since my 0.333 grade point average for that semester meant academic probation was in my immediate future.

Molecular Biology: F. Organic Chemistry: F. Trigonometry: F. Leadership: A. Too bad Leadership was only a one-hour class!

I turned my attention to the University of Arkansas at Monticello (UAM). It was closer to home—just 20 miles north of Fountain Hill. More importantly, the Boll Weevils (yes, that's UAM's mascot) were starting a rodeo team and recruiting cowboys. It was a long shot to make the team, but I planned to give it my best shot.

God had healed my heart and restored my stamina. Physical limitations were no longer a major hindrance. It was time for me to make my return, and physical fitness became my top priority.

Even though my resurgence was in its infancy, I realized the hard work of preparation never ends; hence the Bear Down principle.

In rodeo, cowboys motivate fellow competitors with positive candor. It's unlike any other sport I've witnessed. Imagine an NFL game where both teams were encouraging the kicker to hit a 50-yard field goal to win the game. I don't think so!

Rodeo is different.

Phrases such as "Bear Down," "110," and "Get-a-Holt" are often cheered as cowboys prepare for their next ride. It's a universal cowboy language meaning, "Try your very best."

While these words are often outward expressions of encouragement during live competition, "Bear Down" held a broader meaning for me. It was the code phrase I used to push my personal limits during my preparations. In every workout, every run, and every practice session, I reminded myself that bearing down would one day pay off.

If I was going to bear down at UAM, I needed a spot on the team. Fortunately, Mike Smith, UAM's inaugural rodeo coach, also was the father of my childhood friend Courtney Smith. Even though Courtney was at McNeese State, we managed to keep in touch. So after a few phone calls, I landed an interview with Mike. He knew my background, my medical situation, and my desire to fight bulls and prepare to the best of my abilities.

God had opened another door. Before the interview concluded, I was offered a spot on the team. Coach Smith wanted me to compete in the team roping and tie-down roping events. The newfound opportunity, meanwhile, provided me the gateway to fighting bulls at practice sessions and, ultimately, in collegiate rodeo events.

Despite spending many days, weeks, and months off the path, God was still in control of my life. Transferring to UAM was all part of God's plan. I didn't always understand it. I didn't always see it. I certainly didn't make it easy. Nonetheless, God had been in control the entire time. As it is written in Romans 8:28, "And we know that for those who love God all things work together for good, for those who are called according to His purpose." (ESV)

There is no mention in that truth that suggests things only work for those who are blameless or remain on the path.

Despite my most recent academic performance, or lack thereof, my overall GPA remained above a 2.0. That was good enough for admission into UAM, but the university wasn't showering me with scholarship offers.

Money was still tight.

Coach Smith came through with a rodeo scholarship that cut my tuition in half. I don't know what that says about his judgment, but I was certainly thankful. The remaining bill was paid in part by private scholarships, mostly $500 a pop. Watching me pay for tuition would have made an extreme coupon'r proud.

After settling in on campus, Coach and I frequently discussed my passion for bullfighting. I was interested in making up for lost time. Since the electrocution, I hadn't done much more than dress up as a cowboy for fraternity parties. I hadn't roped or ridden a horse in nearly three years—much less competed at a rodeo or stood in front of a bull!

Even prior to the accident, from the age of 14 to 18, I only fought bulls at my uncle's rodeo and a few amateur rodeos close to home. Including the period I was recovering, that equates to four years tinkering with rodeo and three years sidelined.

My experience was limited, but my desire was endless.

I think this is what God wants from all of us. He wants our desire and obedience, not our ability. Throughout the Bible, example after example shows God using imperfect people for His perfect plan.

Matthew 19:26 provides great hope: "Jesus looked at them and said, 'With man this is impossible, but with God all things are possible!'"(NIV) For me to fulfill my God-given vision of reaching people through bullfighting, clearly I would have to be another example of that truth.

Coach Smith and I implemented an intense physical workout schedule and intentionally built in a spiritual growth plan. Every day, I walked onto the campus football field with a Winston Churchill quote on my mind and Philippians 4:13 in my heart.

The verse promises that, "I can do all things through Him who strengthens me." (ESV) And I believed, without a doubt, that with God all things were possible.

The Churchill quote, meanwhile, served as a daily reminder that my day was coming; I just needed to prepare.

"To each there comes in their lifetime a special moment when they are figuratively tapped on the shoulder and offered the chance to do a very special thing, unique to them and fitted to their talents. What a tragedy if that moment finds them unprepared or unqualified for that which could have been their finest hour."

Before Churchill became the prime minister of the United Kingdom and the man who is celebrated today for his leadership, he knew great defeat. As an example, he lost in a landslide election his first run at office, yet he remained focused, believing that with great preparation his day was coming.

If my day were to come, I knew I had to prepare. So, six days a week, I executed the following:

- Bible reading

- Prayer time

- One-mile warm-up run

- 100 box jumps

- 100 pushups

- 100 sit ups

- 16 120-yard wind sprints

- 15-mile bike ride

- 10 sets of agility drills

On Sundays, I rested with the exception of going to church in Monticello with my Papaw Cruce, reading the Bible, having prayer time, and analyzing bullfighting films. I was a long way from perfect, but the schedule provided guardrails to keep me out of the ditches.

Before long, God transformed me from a patient under medical supervision to a fit athlete. Despite the long road and various distractions, the dream was coming into focus.

I continued to bear down.

Donny continued to encourage me to pursue my dream and challenged me to continue my education.

That was great, but I also needed to move from pep talks to the practice field. If I was going to have any chance to break through, I desperately needed to be schooled in the sport.

THE ART OF BULLFIGHTING

Art McDaniel was still in south Arkansas, but by January 1999, his rodeo career had concluded. He had married a sweet girl he first met at the Malvern rodeo (the night after I ate all of those bananas for his amusement). So while I was settling in at UAM, Art and Laura were settling in to married life and eager to start a family.

I figured he wasn't interested in making a comeback, but I called him anyway.

"Art," I said, "I'm back in town going to UAM, and I need help with my bullfighting."

I didn't need him to make a triumphant return. Just come out of retirement for a little bit, I hoped. Cowboy protection typically involves two fighters in the arena, so I needed him as a partner, but more importantly, as a coach.

"Sparks, you know I'm not rodeoing these days," he said.

We bantered back and forth, and he agreed to fight bulls with me as long as the practices and events were close to home. I think he could hear in my voice that I was serious and genuinely needed his help. I no longer was a star-struck kid talking in dream world.

By the summer, we felt good about my progress. Art and I had rodeo'd close to home, and I had picked up several events in bordering states. While not perfect, my skills improved each day.

By the end of my first year at UAM, I had the opportunity to fight bulls at eight of our 10 regional college rodeos. Our team traveled the collegiate circuit from Arkansas to Michigan and all across the southeastern United States.

Every day, an inch; every week, a foot; and every month, a yard. During the first year at UAM, I made more progress than the aggregate of all my previous years' experiences.

BATTLES OF THE MIND

As I returned to seeking God's will, the devil took notice.

I am confident that anytime God is doing a great work in our lives, the enemy is aware and is strategizing against us. The devil's campaign has one goal—to deter our efforts in fulfilling God's purpose.

At times I wanted to concede. There were crazy thoughts racing in my mind. The devil tried to tell me God couldn't be glorified though me. After all, I was just a small-town kid, a nobody. How could God possibly use me—a complete wreck in great need of God's grace? I was an aspiring rodeo cowboy, not the next Billy Graham. My mind struggled to make sense of my calling.

As those thoughts fled, the paradox shifted. The devil couldn't win with negativity, so he flipped the script. Maybe I was the next best thing, he suggested, called by God to do a mighty work. If so, why had I strayed off the route? Perhaps, the devil implied, I wasn't up to the calling God had given me.

The devil used self-doubt, pride, envy, and unwholesome talk as schemes to derail my journey. Many times I felt all of those irrational feelings at once.

The overwhelming emotional roller coaster made me think occasionally about throwing in the towel.

Spiritual warfare is real. As 2 Corinthians 10:4 states, "For the weapons of our warfare are not of the flesh but have divine power to destroy strongholds." (ESV) The enemy loves to use the desires of our flesh to creep into our life so he can edge God out.

Having witnessed my parents fight on the battlefield of spiritual warfare, I knew that the only way to win was to press into the presence of God. In Ephesians 4, Paul teaches us to "not give the devil a foothold." And later he explains how to fight that battle: By putting on "the full armor of God, so that when the day of evil comes, you may be able to stand your ground, and after you have done everything, to stand." (Ephesians 6:13, NIV)

That armor consists of the belt of truth, the breastplate of righteousness, feet "fitted" with the readiness that comes from the gospel of peace, the shield of faith, the helmet of salvation, and the sword of the Spirit, which is the word of God.

That armor has never failed me, except during the times I have simply chosen not to wear it.

"HUNGARY" FOR LOVE

Satan loved those times, and often used my dating life when he was ready to pounce. I wasn't an aspiring Casanova, but I still made for an easy target.

Donny's advice from the 1998 NFR was both accurate and

precise. For a young guy traveling the rodeo circuit like a car-ney-in-training, I slipped in and out of this "I'm not here for a long time, just a good time" mentality.

In this season of life, I met a Hungarian girl who had come to the United States to play basketball. As destiny would have it, she ended up in Monticello, Arkansas, of all places.

She was as reserved as I was social. She would typically avoid making eye contact with me at all costs. So after one of her basketball games, I decided to introduce myself.

My best friend, Johnathan Walthall, had a class with her and provided the following details: Her name is Kriszti, she is very quiet, she's from Hungary, and she's Catholic.

Of all the corny pickup lines I've used over the years, this was the best one yet, "I wanted to tell you that I really love your country." Without giving her a chance to speak, I kept piling it on. "I went on a mission trip to Hungary."

You could imagine her surprise!

Arkansas is a long way from Hungary and the young, home-sick, black-haired, brown-eyed girl fell for every word I spoke.

"Where in Hungary did you go?" she asked.

The truth? I had never been to Hungary and couldn't even tell you where on Earth you might find it.

"Your capital city," I replied.

"Oh, Budapest!" she said.

"Yes, yes, Budapest!"

Mistake Number One: starting a relationship on a lie.

Mistake Number Two: bringing God into my lie!

A mission trip to Hungary? Really?

Down the slippery slope I sped.

As we spent days and weeks hanging out, she and I inevitably fostered a relationship. I pulled out all of the stops as the lies kept pouring in.

"Check this shirt out," I said while holding up a white button up, short sleeve shirt with a floral pattern across the bottom.

"What about it?" Kriszti replied.

"I got it while in Hungary," I lied.

Despite being puzzled, she finally conceded that it could possibly be from Hungary.

It wasn't until three months into dating that I finally came clean about my "mission trip" and fancy white shirt. Honesty relieved the burden I was carrying and almost cost me the girl I was dating. But she stuck with me, and by the end of the spring semester, we were serious.

Kriszti was visibly homesick, however, so we pooled our money for the airfare, and she returned to Hungary for the summer. Meanwhile, I continued to bear down in my training.

SUMMER LESSONS

I intended to spend the summer training in Martin, Tennessee. My good friends (and aspiring cowboys) Cody Martin and Jeremiah Diffee were attending the University of Tennessee-Martin. They, too, were young and hungry, trying to break into professional rodeo.

As summer plans were being finalized, I called Ronny Sparks to talk bullfighting and training tips. We weren't as close as Donny and I were, but he was a great motivator and dared me to live my dream.

"Somebody's here that wants to talk to you," he said.

I couldn't imagine who was at his place looking for me.

In a cautious yet curious voice I said, "Hello."

From the other end of the phone came a loud and cocky, "What are you doing?"

Turns out it was Mike Matt.

I hadn't talked to Mike since the Monroe Bullfights in 1996, three years prior. We had spoken at the 1998 NFR after Spotted Demon reinjured his ankle, but that wasn't much of a conversation.

As God would arrange, he had stopped by Ronny's place en route to a Wrangler Bullfight somewhere east of the Mississippi River.

We made small talk for a few minutes and then he got to his point.

"How about you go on the road with me this summer?" he said.

He's needing the world's most motivated gear bag toter! I thought.

We decided to meet at the College National Finals Rodeo in Casper, Wyoming. From there, we would continue his rodeo run throughout the summer's end.

The college finals were still a month away, so spending time with Cody and Jeremiah in Tennessee remained a viable option. As a cowboy drifter, my plans were always fluid.

Even though it would only be for a month, it was a good opportunity. They had access to arguably the best coaching staff and resources in college rodeo. I wanted to train with them at UTM, even if only for a few weeks.

Once I arrived, our waking hours consisted of eating day-old corndogs, talking rodeo, and fantasizing about being ProRodeo cowboys.

We lived in an old, run-down house and shared our money to survive. Cody landed a job working the graveyard shift at the Modern Tool and Die Company (MTD) Lawn Mower Factory. He was pretty excited to build riding lawn mowers for minimum wage.

His paycheck kept the lights on and the corndogs coming in.

Needing money to travel with Mike, I asked MTD if there were any openings. To my surprise, the human resources manager was an alumnus of the Pike fraternity I pledged at UCA. He hired me on the spot and set me up with a job working on the assembly line with Cody.

Every 52 seconds, MTD built a new riding lawn mower. It was quite the operation. However, all training was learned on the fly with the line actually producing mowers.

My job was to route two basic wires through a square metal frame, thread two bolts, and install a spring. (The spring was similar in size to a trampoline spring.) The line leader said, "Put your elbow on top of your hip bone and just lift up. That'll pop that sucker into place."

Sounded like good advice for the short term, but after three hours that technique was no longer sustainable.

My hand quivered and spasmed, struggling to load the spring. As my pace slowed, we quickly failed to meet the 52-second standard. A sawed-off little fellow, maybe five-foot even at best, looked up at me and said, "We don't hire blankety, blankety, blank at MTD." He continued, cursing me mercilessly.

I reared back to impose my will and Cody wrestled me away. He knew we needed to keep the lights on at home, and I didn't need to turn this fellow's lights out. As the tempers settled, I decided I didn't need the job after all.

The boss didn't quite understand it when I told him I was preparing to Go West.

Outside of realizing I would always treat others with dignity and respect, the best lesson I learned in Martin was Goal Setting 101.

UTM's Rodeo Coach, John Luthi, invited me to join Cody and Jeremiah in his office late one evening. His walls were plastered with rodeo memorabilia, positive quotes, and family photos. Coach Luthi was college rodeo's version of Lou Holtz.

While sitting in his office, he pulled out a small stack of white printer paper. There were roughly five sheets held together by a single staple. The cover sheet had four words printed across the top: The Wild Idea Sheet. He explained that goals were nothing more than wild ideas with a plan behind them; but without the plan, they remained wild ideas.

Over the next two hours we listened intently as he talked about coaching cowboys to national and world titles. They, too, once had the wild idea of becoming a champion cowboy and looked to Coach to chart the course for their journey.

This all fit hand-in-hand with what Coach Smith had outlined when I transferred to UAM. Plus, it supported my Bear Down principle, suggesting that the hard work of preparation never ends. Add to that equation the will of God and you can become unstoppable.

My goals were clear: Earn my spot in the Professional Rodeo Cowboys Association and graduate from college.

The PRCA is the most prestigious rodeo association in the world. Just as the National Football League is the benchmark for football, the PRCA is the measuring stick for rodeo cowboys. Big rodeos with rich history and tradition, such as Cheyenne, San Antonio, Salinas, and so on, are all PRCA rodeos. Earning membership into the PRCA is a rigorous process requiring a financial investment and an evaluation of skills in the arena.

Under each primary goal, we were taught to identify specific, measurable, and obtainable supporting goals. Without supporting goals, it was still just a wild idea on paper.

Once completed, our goal sheets were posted throughout the house, in our car, in every notebook, and in every day planner we owned.

We encouraged each other daily to bear down and give 110 percent.

Here's my rodeo goal sheet:

Goal: Earn My PRCA Card	
Mental	**Physical**
Mentor session/ weekly	Run 10 miles/week
Read one mental prep book/quarter	Bike ride 100 miles/week
10 hours of film study/week	Agility drills 3/week
15 min of mental imagery/day	100 pushups/ sit ups/day

We couldn't even brush our teeth without seeing each other's goals. Then again, we could have lived without brushing our teeth. But there was no way that we could fathom not reaching our goals and fulfilling our purpose in life.

There was a prescribed sequence of events that had to transpire before my goals would be obtained. While not always understanding the struggle, the path, or the reasons why, I was confident that preparation inched me closer. Instead of eat, pray, love, it was practice, study, pray—repeat!

There were no off days in Martin, Tennessee. But as quickly as the days came, they passed. It was now time to meet up with Mike Matt for Bullfighting 101.

PROFESSOR MIKE

As a two-time world champion, Mike was the coach I desperately needed. He schooled me in the art of bullfighting as we traveled countless miles across the United States. Every mile brought a new learning opportunity.

Mike gained a heck of a gear bag toter, and I gained insight, access, and training that money could not buy.

There is no good explanation of how we became fast friends. He was quiet, cocky, and a world champion. I was jovial, inexperienced, and, as Mike put it, "Naïve to the ways of the world."

The one thing we did share in common was a relentless determination to succeed. Although slow to admit it, Mike appreciated my youthful outlook. My hunger to learn increased his appetite to teach. The arena was his classroom and, for me, getting unrestricted access to the professor was priceless.

My confidence increased, I polished my fundamental skills, and I witnessed firsthand the successes that follow hard work.

When the summer run ended, we'd been in Utah, Idaho, Wyoming, Colorado, and Nevada. Mike encouraged me to remain focused on the basics and to plan to declare for the PRCA evaluation process the following year. Earning my PRCA card was looking like a real possibility.

How awesome is it to look back and see God's hand in it all:

- If I hadn't gotten electrocuted

- Had I not received the scholarship to UCA

- If Uncle Jerry hadn't found JIT

- Had I not been around to go with JR to Monroe

- Had Mike not entered the bullfight in Monroe

- If I hadn't called Ronny the one day that Mike was passing through

- If Mike hadn't extended his invitation for me to travel with him

That's a God-inspired sequence of events!

Without a doubt, where God calls, He provides. Those aren't my words; that's God's promise!

He will make a way, we simply prepare for the day.

SOMEBODY'S WATCHING

Over the next year, I fought bulls at 40 events across the southeast. The biggest, of course, was the Rex Dunn Invitational in Lawton, Oklahoma, where Nasty took advantage of me.

Between Donny's steady encouragement, Mike's coaching, and Art's reinforcement, the ability to advance to the professional ranks was nearing reality. Stepping out on faith, it was now time to apply for the PRCA evaluation.

The assessment is similar to a traditional athlete declaring for the draft by competing in a combine camp.

A few things had to happen for an athlete to be considered for a PRCA Bullfighter's Card. You had to fill out an application form and pay a $500 evaluation fee. You had to provide professional endorsements. And you had to list five amateur rodeos you would be working.

Oh, yeah, and include a life insurance beneficiary…just in case. I mailed the application and money order to 101 ProRodeo Drive, Colorado Springs, CO. My brother Jeff was still my number one fan. He spotted me $500 and assured me it was money well invested.

The PRCA would dispatch an evaluator to one of the five events listed on the application. His sole purpose was to grade the candidate's performance, gauging his ability to compete at the highest level. Throughout the process, the evaluator typically remains anonymous, avoiding communication at all costs.

After the evaluation, the applicant receives a letter noting the event where you were evaluated and whether you passed or failed. Only if you passed would you be eligible for membership.

So there I was, in Marshall, Missouri, working the Missouri Valley College Rodeo. Alongside me was Big Ron Craver, the "Cowboy Life Saver." Ron was a battle-tested bullfighter who had succeeded in the professional ranks. As Father Time caught him, he transitioned to mainly working rodeos close to his home. He knew everyone in the business so when he spotted a fellow from the PRCA, he put two and two together.

After 10 or so bulls, Ron pulled me to the side and whispered in my ear.

"You are doing great," he said. "You are being watched."

He didn't have to say anything else; I knew what he meant.

My day had come.

Understanding the weight and magnitude of the situation, I started to recite Philippians 4:13, and replay conversations that Donny and I had shared over the years. I recalled Donny saying, *I did* have the ability to fight bulls. I *would* make it one day.

In Donny's honor, at the end of the event, I hurdled the tallest bull I had ever tried to jump. And by the grace of God, I landed on my feet!

My evaluation was complete.

When the mail arrived three weeks later, I was ecstatic to receive the PRCA's correspondence. I tore open the letter and skimmed the words until I read, APPROVED! What a great moment.

When my day came, I was prepared.

COWBOY LOGIC

1. What are you currently working on as if it depends on you, while praying as if it depends on God?

2. How do you combat spiritual warfare?

3. What goals do you need to map out to help guide you to your purpose?

And my God will supply every need of yours according to His riches in glory in Christ Jesus.

Philippians 4:19 (ESV)

Arm Candy

Paying the price for taking the bull away from the rider at
the 2007 College National Finals Rodeo in Casper, Wyoming.

Photo by Dan Hubbell

SECTION TWO
The Rocky Road

chapter 5

DUTY CALLS

Principle No. 4: Shoot the Gap—To Sacrifice Is to Live

There are times in the arena when the bulls seem like they're moving in slow motion—when your every move seems to work and nothing can go wrong.

Then, BAM! Without warning, it's as if someone has pushed the fast-forward button on the remote control that is your life. Everything moves too quickly, and you find you are headed in directions you never expected.

That sort of sums up the year 2001—probably for a lot of people, but certainly for me.

When the spring semester rolled around, I was walking in tall cotton. I had my ProRodeo card, the emotional roller coaster had leveled out, and life was good.

Kriszti and I were getting along great, and she was the leading scorer for the UAM women's basketball team. So we were both starting to realize our dreams.

My compass was recalibrated and I was, for the most part, back on track.

My grades at UAM also were more in line with what Mom and Dad expected. I had transformed from a distracted student at UCA into a focused student at UAM, earning all-American scholar honors and other assorted academic accolades.

Success in the arena and classroom opened doors on campus. Like any collegiate athlete, frequent travel required me to miss a fair amount of lectures. But Dr. Dennis Travis, the vice chancellor of academic affairs, ensured that my professors accommodated my busy rodeo schedule.

The university also granted me access to the sports medicine staff, providing a dedicated athletic trainer. His main responsibility was to focus on rehabilitation and recovery. This was vital for a full-contact sport, ensuring my body was ready for the next event.

And the athletic department gave me a key for the fitness center. The liberty to train around the clock and fit customized workouts into my already compacted rodeo and class schedules was a blessing.

By now, Mike Smith had moved on and Mike Galpin led our team. Even through the staffing change, our team remained close-knit. We traveled 10 extended weekends per year, carpooling from Arkansas to Michigan. Despite my rise to the professional level, I was still one of the guys. We were simply cowboys living our dream.

While not lucrative, college rodeo athletes are allowed to keep any money won or earned. This is vastly different from NCAA-regulated sports. I typically earned $750 to $1,000 per event for fighting 30-40 bulls. Not bad money since the school paid all my expenses.

Outside of college rodeos, I worked 10 professional and 20 amateur events from Illinois to Kentucky. While the pros paid more, I had to cover my expenses.

Even with the steady travel, I was on track to graduate in May 2001. I thought: *If I could just get that diploma, a full-time professional rodeo career was near.*

At least that was my plan.

But God had a different idea. He would use the next year to teach me the real value of service above self. I needed to learn how to trust Him, both through His detours and through my poor decisions.

One of the people God used in my life during this time was Dr. Travis. He was an avid runner, and most nights we met in passing on the campus track. In between my wind sprints, we'd end up talking, and he soon took a personal interest in my career aspirations.

"It is remarkable that you can balance your rodeo schedule and academic schedule while excelling in both," he often said.

In reality, he was also due credit for my successes because he was responsible for orchestrating the academic flexibility that the university approved. On the rare occasion a professor didn't support my cause, he paid them a personal visit.

Dr. Travis was a great leader on campus. His calling was helping others fulfill their goals in higher education. He noticed my raw potential and selflessly poured himself into my life.

One night after running, he asked me, "What do you really want to do in your future?"

In an overconfident tone, I said, "Dr. Travis, you know I'm going to rodeo."

He knew that, but he believed something else was hidden within me: A leadership quality that I needed to refine.

Dr. Travis believed the United States military provided the world's best leadership training. His father-in-law served during World War II, and he often spoke with great admiration for his service and sacrifice.

"One of my biggest regrets is not serving in the military," he told me.

I thought, *Okay, but how does that impact me?*

Dr. Travis continued. "Jeremy, you are a natural leader. I think you would do very well as a military officer."

I became pretty annoyed. How dare someone suggest that my plans included anything outside of full-time rodeoing?

The military didn't appeal to me in the least. My focus was to earn the 16 credit hours that stood between me and a college degree. I wanted to leave the graduation stage and head down the rodeo trail.

ADOPTING SACRIFICE

Chasing a world title was my ultimate dream. In 2000, the PRCA selected me and a handful of rookies for a freestyle bullfight at the Benny Binion's Stock Sale. The sale was an opportunity for top rookies to showcase their talents in conjunction with the National Finals Rodeo. Placing second motivated me even more.

I was dead set on pursuing a world title the following season. Unfortunately, the Wrangler Bullfighting Tour folded just a week later. Mike Matt won his third title that December and will forever be the last Wrangler World Champion Bullfighter.

With that, my aspirations to compete in freestyle events started to fade. Since there was no longer an opportunity to be a world champion, I thought, *What is the point of freestyle bullfighting?*

As winter turned to spring, I began to embrace the cowboy protection aspect of bullfighting. I was improving with every performance, and I started to see the importance of sacrificing for others.

Someone laying down their life to save another is a beautiful picture. Without any regard for their own body or personal well-being, individuals have jumped on grenades, battled terrorists on foreign soil, and disarmed people committed to wreaking havoc on mankind.

Much like the three friends who charged, tackled, and subdued the terrorist on the Paris-bound train in 2015, ordinary people have made, and will continue to make, selfless sacrifices.

These acts are visible, commendable, and clearly needed.

In cowboy protection, a bullfighter willingly stands in the gap to take a direct blow from an angry bull. All for the sake of protecting a fleeing bull rider who clearly needs safety.

"Shooting the gap" is the bullfighting term that describes this action. The purpose is to wedge in between a charging bull and a fallen rider. We live for these moments. Until we're needed, we are unrecognizable and simply blend into the surroundings. But at a moment's notice, when called to action, we shoot the gap and mitigate the crisis or even take the hit.

The best bullfighters effortlessly slip in and out of dangerous situations. The display of visual love and sacrifice for a fellow man is awe-inspiring. I believe it's a calling that brings glory to God— demonstrating that there is no greater love than to sacrifice yourself for someone else.

Placing such a strong value on sacrifice, I realized the need to live the Shoot the Gap principle. It suggests that to sacrifice is to live. I had always seen sacrifice through the lens of what you gave up. I thought to sacrifice for something was to die for it. Now I understand sacrifice isn't always death; sometimes you sacrifice to live, because selflessly serving the needs of others brings purpose and joy to your life.

In a sport where extreme courage is required, visible sacrifices are persistent. That's the premise for a bullfighter's role. Most of my career was spent preparing for the moment I would be called to action.

While working a college rodeo in Murray, Kentucky, this idea that to sacrifice is to live was tested. It was one of those "life in fast-forward" moments.

A bull rider was tossed, but his hand remained trapped in his rope. In addition to being hung up, he was violently thrashed to the ground. His body was in a vulnerable position, in danger of being trampled. The bull wasn't horrifying, but he was rather heavy, maybe 1,800 pounds, and had large clown stabbers (horns).

My instincts took over. I didn't necessarily feel threatened or experience fear. My only thought was freeing the rider. As I reached for the rider's hand and grabbed the tail of his rope to set him free, the bull whipped his head around, catching me in the groin with his left horn.

The force vaulted me into the air.

Flying uncontrollably, I managed to maintain my grip on the rope and thankfully free the rider.

The adrenaline was overwhelming. Without question, I was hurt. My left leg didn't move on command. Standing was impossible. It took all of my upper-body strength to crawl to safety and avoid being trampled.

As soon as the bull exited the arena, help rushed to my aid.

Blood covered my lower extremities.

The medics revealed a 2-inch-deep puncture wound in my groin. But, as any cowboy would, I refused to go to the ER. I wasn't sure of my condition, but figured my $1,000 paycheck wasn't going to cover it!

Sacrifice was a part of the job, and I was ecstatic that both of us were able to live to see another day.

CAPPED AND GOWNED

The excitement of graduation permeated throughout our family that May. Friends and relatives made plans to witness the milestone event. Kriszti wasn't graduating until December, but her parents were flying over from Hungary and would attend as well.

My mom, Aunt Dian Ricks, Uncle John Ricks, and several cousins were UAM alumni. So a family homecoming was fast approaching.

Just days prior to graduation, Dr. Travis stopped by the track to check in.

"Jeremy, would you go with me to the university's job fair next week?" he asked.

"Dr. Travis, I'm not interested in a job," I told him, "I'm a cowboy!"

"Well, would you at least join me when I make my rounds?" he asked.

"Sure, Dr. Travis," I agreed out of obligation.

While I'm not the smartest person, I am smart enough to listen to smart people. Dr. Travis sang my praises at every booth in the fair. He was proud of me, and he was sure my work ethic in sports was transferable.

I was offered two jobs on the spot. And on the spot, I turned them down. I was there out of respect for Dr. Travis, not in search of a job.

As we headed out, Dr. Travis stopped by the armed forces recruiting tables to make small talk. Before long, he was pitching me to the recruiters.

Come on, Dr. Travis, I thought. *You're killing me!*

"Dennis Travis," he said as he extended his hand to the Air Force recruiter.

"Master Sgt. Ralph Hornsby, United States Air Force," was the reply.

"Master Sgt. Hornsby, this is Jeremy Sparks," Dr. Travis continued. "He is graduating next week *magna cum laude*. He's a professional bullfighter and has done a tremendous job representing our university."

There was no way I was going into the military. In fact, my high school senior yearbook posed the following question: "What is the one thing that you will not do?" I answered, "Join the military!" The notion of structure wasn't ideal for this cowboy drifter.

As politely as possible, I told the master sergeant that a military career didn't interest me.

"Jeremy, if you change your mind, let me know," he said. "The Air Force could use a bullfighter."

He gave me his business card and we departed the job fair.

Dr. Travis continued to encourage me to consider the Air Force in the days leading to graduation. I agreed to take the Air Force Officer Qualifying Test (AFOQT), but my focus was on rodeo.

In that world, I was gaining traction. While I hadn't experienced a major breakthrough, I was starting to make a name for myself. I was graduating with honors yet choosing rodeo over corporate America, so the *ProRodeo Sports News (PSN)*, the PRCA's official publication, profiled my story.

"Jeremy Sparks has one of the most impressive lists of academic accomplishments in ProRodeo," the article said.

As I was graduating from college, Sean Graves, a staff sergeant in the Air Force, was reading the *PSN* from his duty location in New Jersey. He, too, was an aspiring bullfighter, and he was in need of a coach. After reading the story, he located my contact information online and sent me an email about bullfighting. He signed it "Gravy"—his military call sign.

Interesting, I thought. *My journey has been anything but "gravy"!*

He asked to fly to Arkansas to work with me on his fundamentals. Knowing how many people had invested in me, who was I to deny helping Gravy?

He scheduled his military leave for early September and prepared to attend Bullfighting 101.

I met Sean at the Little Rock airport on September 8. After a quick introduction, we loaded his bags and headed south to Cruces. Gravy's only goal for the week was to fight as many bulls as possible. We were like-minded and had similar aspirations, so we immediately hit it off.

We woke up the morning of September 11 and began preparing breakfast. Mom turned on the TV and tuned into the only channel that came through in Fountain Hill. Regardless of how many channels were broadcasting across the United States that morning, only one story was showing.

What a helpless feeling we experienced as we stood around the TV and watched as terrorists flew hijacked airliners into the Twin Towers in New York, the Pentagon in Washington, D.C., and a field in Pennsylvania. *How did such cowardly acts happen on our home soil?*

Gravy contacted his duty station, McGuire Air Force Base, New Jersey. His commander told him to report to duty immediately, and Sean caught the first flight home after commercial airlines resumed operation.

Just like that, he was off to prepare to fight terrorists—anytime, anyplace.

I believe Sean's trip to Arkansas that particular week was providential. It changed my heart, my thinking—and my course.

Here was a guy who wanted nothing more than to try his hand at rodeo. The very moment the first plane crashed into the World Trade Center, we were all changed. But Gravy reinforced the notion that to sacrifice is to live. Gravy's eyes revealed the price he was willing to pay. It far exceeded anything that I could fathom.

In our living room stood a true American patriot.

On the way home from dropping him off at the airport, I found myself moved beyond words. For a moment, I thought back to the recruiters at the job fair. Master Sgt. Hornsby had said the Air Force needed a bullfighter.

What are the chances of that really happening? I thought.

At most, it was likely just another sales pitch to hit a quota. No professional bullfighter, or even a professional cowboy, for that matter, had ever represented the United States Air Force while also serving in its ranks. Yet, I felt moved to continue exploring the possibility. It would be a complete reversal of my original plan, but clearly in line with Shooting the Gap.

I rang Master Sgt. Hornsby's office 30 minutes after wrestling with the idea. Somewhere between Little Rock and Pine Bluff, he picked up. Sean's reaction to 9/11 impacted me to the core, and my heart began to pour out.

"I want to do more," I told the recruiter. "I want to serve."

Even if serving meant putting my dream on hold, I was committed.

But Hornsby was intrigued by the idea having a bullfighting Air Force officer. So he promised to research the possibilities. We were about to find out the chances of having a bullfighter serve in the Air Force.

Although I had taken the AFOQT, I had to formally interview for Officer Training School (OTS). On the OTS application, potential trainees were asked to list their top three preferred career fields and top five duty stations. Mine read, "Needs of Service," followed by Langley, Virginia, Little Rock, Arkansas, and few other southern bases.

The pride that Dr. Travis had shown when talking about his father-in-law was becoming personal.

THE AIRMAN'S CREED

On September 28, 2001, I raised my right hand and swore to support and defend the United States against all enemies, foreign and domestic.

My parents didn't really like this idea. War was imminent. Their thoughts about me leaving for the service were similar to their thoughts when I started fighting bulls—they were worried about my life.

But, again, Mom and Dad committed to being dedicated prayer warriors, interceding on my behalf for safety and protection.

I reported to OTS on October 1, 2001 and had my eyes opened to the discipline required of future leaders in the world's most powerful air force. Starting day one, the experience was a blur. We trained long and hard, averaging 16 hours each day for 90 days. It was physically and mentally draining, but, as with my commitment to bullfighting, seeing the progress was rewarding.

Even under pressure, I sought to encourage others, using humor and cowboy logic. At times, it kept our unit moving forward. Much like when I was working on the farm, I was always open to a good laugh!

One evening, I noticed a spider hanging in mid-air as our unit stood at attention (heels together making a V-shape, a roll of quarters in each hand with thumbs pointed down, back straight, and butt cheeks clenched together).

We were under the foyer of the dining facility and our flight training officer, 1st Lt. Gabel, kept a watchful eye on us as we waited eagerly for our scheduled chow time. Lt. Gabel stood next to me and was directly beneath the eight-legged creature. As the spider inched closer, roughly an inch from his shoulder, I broke the position of attention—a real no-no for a trainee. Reaching out with my right hand, I quickly grabbed what appeared to be a black widow.

"OT (Officer Trainee) Sparks, what are you doing breaking the position of attention?" Lt. Gabel barked.

"Sir, I just saved your life."

The spider was still in my hand. However, I was more concerned about the lieutenant punishing me for breaking attention than I was about a spider bite.

"OT Sparks," he said, "What do you deserve for saving my life?"

I wasn't sure what I was entitled to, but I figured an achievement ribbon of some sort was in my future. Then again, it was only a lieutenant's life!

"Sir, I deserve one piece of pie," I replied.

Desserts were off limits for trainees. Yet the cooks set them out every meal. It felt like cruel and unusual punishment. A little comfort food would have gone a long way on the hard 16-hour days.

We only had three minutes to eat, so adding dessert would likely mean busting our time limit. But it was a risk I was willing to take. Anything for a piece of homemade pie.

Lt. Gabel agreed.

"OT Sparks, you earned one piece of pie for saving my life," he said. My smile beamed from ear to ear as the other trainees looked on in amazement.

Thinking the situation was settled, I released the spider.

And as it fell to the ground, I once again heard the lieutenant's voice.

"OT Sparks," he yelled, "did you just litter my floor?"

"Yes, Sir," I said.

"Do you start your sentences with yes?" he asked. I knew better—everything started with Sir.

"Sir, yes, Sir," I said, trying to recover. "I littered on your floor."

He was beyond fired up.

"I don't want a sir sandwich," he shouted. "OT Sparks, since you littered on my floor, you will not get any pie."

I couldn't believe it, I'd saved this man's life, and he was mad about me leaving a biodegradable spider on concrete!

It took about a month of training, but I eventually grew accustomed to marching, eating fast, being yelled at, and moving with a sense of urgency. It was a game. Learning how to play by their rules was a necessary evil.

After observing my leadership style and ability to motivate, encourage, and entertain, Lt. Gabel appointed me as our unit's chaplain. The unique mission was a perfect fit for my calling. I welcomed the opportunity to witness, encourage, serve, and testify. Even though I was nowhere close to a rodeo, God was still using me as a vessel for His will.

Soon, word spread across the training base that I was a professional bullfighter. The instructors liked to see how tough I was, and various military media outlets researched my story. The *Air Force News*, *Air Force Crossroads*, the *Leader Magazine*, and a few other military publications scheduled time to meet with me.

By the time instructors were done yelling at me, there wasn't much time for interviews, but they made it happen. In total, six sessions were scheduled over that 12-week training period. All of the reporters asked the same question: "Why serve?"

"I realized that I needed to do my part for the country," was my consistent answer.

To sacrifice is to live.

COWBOY LOGIC

1. What sacrifices have you made for your family, friends, co-workers, or country?

2. Describe a time when you ended up doing what you thought you would never do.

3. How do you define sacrifice?

Greater love has no one than this, that someone lay down his life for his friends.

John 15:13 (ESV)

chapter 6
DIVINE ASSIGNMENT

Principle No. 5: EGO—Humility Is a True Reflection of Strength

We rarely got to use the phones at Officer Training School. In fact, the phones were off limits except on Saturdays. Even then, we could only make one call (as long as demerits didn't restrict the privilege).

Kriszti typically hung out at my parents' place on Saturdays. This afforded me the opportunity to talk with everyone at once. So on the Saturday when we all learned where we'd be going and what we'd be doing after OTS, I was eager to call and share the news.

Roughly 20 sheets of loose-leaf paper were posted on the wall beside the pay phones. We'd been training hard for eight weeks, and everyone desperately wanted to learn their first job and duty location.

Knowing that I had listed "Needs of Service" for my job, I was extremely curious to learn my career field. There were approximately 150 Air Force Specialty Codes (AFSC). With the exception of professional and aviation-related jobs, the vast majority of AFSCs were in play.

I also was excited to learn where I would be assigned. I liked my chances of staying in the south. All five bases I had listed as a personal preference were south of the Mason Dixon line. But, again, that was my preference, not Uncle Sam's guarantee.

In bold ink, I found my identification number followed by "Jeremy A. Sparks, Personnel, F.E. Warren AFB, Wyoming."

What?!

Personnel in the Air Force is much like human resources in the civilian sector. Since my degree was in communications and I enjoyed working with people, I thought, *Personnel is a decent fit.*

But, Wyoming?

Where did that come from? I didn't list Wyoming on my application. I certainly didn't leave any blanks for duty assignments either. In permanent ink, I listed five southern states. What could have happened?

Then it hit me: God had a plan. My job was to simply trust, as faith makes all things possible.

I called home with the same sense of urgency I had while marching. As soon as my folks picked up the phone, I blurted out, "I'm getting stationed in Wyoming!"

Random thoughts flooded my mind.

OTS graduation is in December. Kriszti is graduating from UAM in December. Do we get married? Do we break up? Does she go back to Hungary? Or does she stay in the U.S. and play basketball?

An F3 mental tornado swirled in my mind.

We had just a few weeks to sort it all out. The anxiety of being stationed so far from home added another layer of uncertainty. I felt rushed in sharing this news. There wasn't much time to think, talk, or act. Other trainees had calls to make and loved ones to inform.

I asked to speak to Kriszti in private.

She took the phone and paced the floor, while I remained surrounded by 100 of my closest friends.

"What are you doing January 5th?" I asked.

"I have no idea," she said. "Why?"

In retrospect, I was operating in emotional overload and hadn't fully considered the ramifications of my next words.

"Well, if we are going to get married," I said, "I only have January 5th free."

"Are you asking me to marry you?" she replied.

"I guess so," I said with a lump in my throat and trepidation in my heart.

She said, "Yes."

CHILLY FEET

On December 20, 2001, after three long months at Maxwell Air Force Base in Montgomery, Alabama, I graduated OTS.

Earning a commission as a United States Air Force Second Lieutenant was a pretty nice feeling. Never again did I want to hear, "Get out of bed! Get out of bed! OT Sparks, you better be moving!"

I returned to my parents' home after graduation and began frantically planning our wedding and our move to Wyoming. I spent much of that time in the same room where I had my God-inspired dream; however, He seemed pretty distant as I rushed to make the wedding a reality.

The ceremony was to be simple. Little Rock Air Force Base still had Christmas decorations hung. The Honor Guard was available to conduct a military wedding. My brother (a pastor) would officiate, and my sister-in-law would sing. Other than paying a pianist and picking up our wedding bands, there weren't any other costs.

How easy, I thought.

As the wedding day approached, the ol' mental tornado started to swirl. Haste had caused my mouth to outrun my brain and redemption day was near. But something wasn't right. My stomach was in knots; I felt ill.

Mom noticed. She had those motherly instincts. It was obvious to her that I was burdened.

"What is wrong with you?" she asked.

"Nothing, Momma," I mumbled. "I'm fine."

For the last three months, self-discipline had been beaten into my skull. I had too much pride to admit concern.

Kriszti's parents had flown to Arkansas. She was the first of their kids to marry. It took a good portion of their savings to finance the trip. Knowing their sacrifice only added to my nausea.

I am solely responsible for this, I thought.

Mom continued pressing for the truth.

"Jeremy, tell Momma what's wrong," she said in a concerned tone that only a mother speaks.

Holding it in was only making matters worse. I had to release my angst.

Fighting back the tears, I confessed.

"Mom, I don't think I want to get married," I said.

Mom loved me unconditionally. Her wisdom always came from a place of authenticity. Sure enough, she leaned in, wrapped her arms around my back, and hugged me tight.

"Jeremy, you don't have to get married," she said with great empathy.

In my mind, that wasn't the case. I didn't see any way around it. *I have to go through with this*, I thought.

I couldn't fathom canceling the day of the wedding.

"It would be better to call it off today than later down the road," she said.

That was solid advice. And, in hindsight, it's easy to see the troubled waters we were about to enter. We were from different cultures. We had different priorities and different passions. We had different theologies—I was a grace-focused evangelical Christian, while she held fast to a more traditional works-based view of Catholicism.

In my position, however, Mom's wisdom was easy to understand yet impossible to apply. So we followed through and wed.

THE COWBOY STATE

As soon as we said "I do," we climbed into the moving van and started the 1,164-mile trek to Wyoming, home of Yellowstone National Park, Grand Teton National Park, and, of course, Francis E. Warren Air Force Base.

It's also home to the Cheyenne Frontier Days Rodeo (CFD).

The rodeo is known as the "Daddy of 'Em All." In fact, it is the largest outdoor western celebration in the world, dating back to 1897. Over the last nine days of every July, the population of Cheyenne grows from around 60,000 to more than 200,000, with people from around the world making the pilgrimage to watch the Wild West come to life.

Not knowing how long we would be stationed at F.E. Warren, I immediately updated my rodeo goals. Just like every goal I'd set since my time in Martin, Tennessee, I wrote down the main objective: "Fight bulls at CFD one time before PCSing." (PCS is the military acronym for a Permanent Change of Station.)

It was a stretch goal, for sure, requiring divine intervention. Still, believing that faith makes all things possible, I knew that if it was God's will, He would make a way.

The first time I shared my goal with someone outside of my family, I was almost laughed out of town. Our financial advisor was a prior CFD Chairman and his office was plastered with CFD memorabilia. Thinking it was a pro-CFD environment, I shared my new goal.

His reaction? Well, to paraphrase, he said, "No way. Dream on."

He didn't realize my God moved mountains.

I didn't realize my God would use this goal to teach me another principle: The strength of humility. To understand humility fully, I had to go around the world. Learning it and living it, however, were two very different challenges.

TO KOREA AND BACK

In March, Mr. Lee Jong-Pill with the South Korean Culture and Tourism Ministry invited me to perform at the Cheongdo Bullfighting Festival. Just as God arranged my assignment to Cheyenne, He opened this door, as well. Other than a Google search for "rodeo bullfighters," there's not a good explanation for how Mr. Lee found me.

After some research and negotiations, the South Korean Minister of Tourism and my Air Force chain of command finalized plans for me to travel to South Korea. The mission was simple: Perform an American-style exhibition bullfight.

I had a few raw nerves about going overseas. The most concerning was the fact I'd never been over the seas! For the sake of my sanity and safety, I negotiated to have a fellow American join me on the adventure.

Mike Matt was the first person I thought would like to share in this experience. Even as a three-time world champion, he had never been afforded an international opportunity. He agreed and we quickly packed our bags.

Cheongdo is Asia's most acclaimed bullfighting festival. It's a sight to behold—an event full of culture, entertainment, and pageantry. Bullfighting in Korea is similar to cockfighting in America. Two bulls fight head-to-head until one quits.

Mike and I performed our exhibition bullfight on two consecutive days using local bulls. The Korean bulls are trained to respect humans and fight other bulls. Their aggression toward us was mild—nothing like the aggressive American freestyle bullfights we'd hoped to showcase.

An estimated 300,000 people, including the president of South Korea, watched us perform. From Fountain Hill to South Korea, I was standing on one of the largest bullfighting stages in the world.

While shaking hands with their president, I thought, *God is good.*

The media took notice of our performance, featuring us in every major South Korean news medium. The story was picked up by Armed Forces media outlets around the globe, quickly making its way back to F.E. Warren.

When we returned home, Lt Col. James "Jim" Carrol, assistant to the CFD General Committee, called my office.

"I read an article about you performing in Korea," he said. "Have you ever thought about performing at Cheyenne Frontier Days?"

"Every day since I was 14 years old!" I said in an overzealous, yet awe-shucks tone. "Sir, is this a joke?"

Some of the greatest bullfighters in the world never get to perform at Cheyenne.

Lt. Col. Carrol was stoic in his response.

"No, it isn't a joke," he said. "Let me see what I can do."

Colonel Don Kidd was the CFD Military Chairman responsible for coordinating the U.S. Thunderbirds, medics, and military volunteers for the event. If there was a way for me to connect with CFD, Col. Kidd was in the perfect position.

Shortly after he discussed the potential opportunity with the general committee, I received another call. This time it was from the CFD Contestant Chairman, Tom Hirsig. Tom was ultimately responsible for the rodeo portion of the western celebration.

"If the senior bullfighter agrees for you to join the bullfighting team," he said, "I'm good with you fighting bulls on military appreciation day."

The senior bullfighter at CFD was none other than world champion Rick Chatman. I knew Rick Chatman! I annoyed the heck out of him 11 years earlier back in Little Rock, Arkansas. He even signed a picture for me that day!

So I called him up and said just that. "Rick, this is Jeremy Sparks. We met in 1991 in Little Rock. You signed a picture for me while visiting at the state fair!"

"Jeremy," he said, "how've you been?"

Rick didn't remember me from a hole in the wall. Nonetheless, I began to share the unique proposition.

I explained the situation just as Tom had explained it to me. His reply was a testament to his humble position. The world champion said, "Jeremy, I will do anything that brings credit to Cheyenne Frontier Days."

When we hung up, I immediately called Tom and enthusiastically repeated Rick's reaction. "Rick told me he supports anything that brings credit to Cheyenne."

"Congratulations!" Tom said. I could hear in his voice that he, too, understood the impact Cheyenne makes on cowboys, young and old, rookies and world champions.

TRUE STRENGTH

In a matter of months, God took me from being a rookie with a stretch goal, to serving as the 11th bullfighter in the history of CFD. It was like a recently drafted pitcher being called to the majors just in time to pitch in the playoffs.

Ty Murray, the world champion bull rider and all-around hand known as the "King of the Cowboys," compares Cheyenne to Lambeau Field, Madison Square Garden, and Wrigley Field.

"It's probably the most famous, historic venue that rodeos are held in," Murray said in 2010 when interviewed by the *Wyoming*

Tribune Eagle. "So you know that when you ride there, every person that was anyone in the sport has competed there. And you just feel it. It's like you feel the ghosts when you ride there...when you know all the cool history that has been played out in that dirt, to have played a small part in that is pretty cool."

A principle was added to my core values as a result of that experience. In a sport where self-promotion and ego ran rampant, Rick was totally fine with sharing the stage with a rookie. He understood that life wasn't meant for selfish desires.

"Ego" for me now stood for Edging God Out—a subtle reminder hidden in Principle No. 5: Humility is a true reflection of strength.

Performing at Cheyenne was sensory overload. The arena is the biggest in the industry. The stadium seats 19,000 people, and live action covers every square foot. On military appreciation day, the arena was filled to capacity. The patriotic flare following 9/11 was intense.

My heart pounded as the national anthem rang out.

Fireworks lit up the sky to kick off that 2002 Cheyenne Frontier Days performance.

When rodeo announcer Justin McKee introduced me as "Lt. Jeremy Sparks, Air Force officer and professional bullfighter," people went nuts. Most of the fans had never heard of me, but they appreciated the sacrifice of men and women in uniform that I represented.

For the next three hours, the greatest rodeo in the history of our sport unfolded. Over 450 cowboys and cowgirls competed on that Wild West, July afternoon, including 60 bull riders.

And all 60 walked away unscathed.

When the performance concluded, the CFD chairmen praised my performance. While I had room to improve, there was no denying my enthusiasm and effort. I was like a teenager test-driving a corvette. The pedal stayed on the metal as I worked to help protect every rider.

Before taking off my gear at the end of the day, Tom Hirsig contracted me to return the following year. The agreement proposed that I could perform at CFD as long as I desired. For a rookie, this was unchartered territory and humbling, to say the least.

Establishing a legacy at CFD became my new goal.

CHANGING ASSIGNMENTS

Shortly after my first performance at CFD, my chain of command, starting with my squadron commander, all the way up to my major command commander, worked tirelessly with the Pentagon and ultimately helped secure my endorsement. "Case 05-195" was the file name with the signed contract that made it official. I was now the only professional bullfighter in U.S. Air Force history. As you can imagine, a lot of obstacles had to be overcome. More than one senior leader had to be convinced that an Air Force bullfighter was somehow a good idea.

What Master Sgt. Hornsby had proposed at the UAM job fair came to fruition 16 months later.

In 2004, Kriszti and I relocated to Vandenberg Air Force Base, California to attend the Air Force's Space and Missile school. Before the school started, my follow-on assignment was to the 2nd Space Operations Squadron (2SOPS) in Colorado Springs. Their mission was flying GPS satellites. Pretty futuristic stuff.

Two months in, the Air Force Personnel Center (AFPC) called. AFPC was responsible for officer assignments. I thought, *Why in the world are they calling me? I already have my orders.*

A stranger's voice cut to the chase.

"Lt. Sparks," he said, "as a professional bullfighter representing the Air Force, we believe it is best that you be reassigned to Cheyenne. Your orders to 2SOPS have been revoked. You will now serve as an ICBM Combat Crew Member at F.E. Warren."

Being a "Missileer" meant holding the keys to the world's most powerful weapon system. On paper, it seemed pretty glamorous. Flight suits, leather bomber jackets, and an active role supporting war fighters around the globe.

In reality, two officers reside in a capsule roughly 30-feet long by eight-feet wide using Cold War-era technology to operate 10 nuclear missiles.

Not necessarily futuristic.

I knew the mission of strategic deterrence and strike-force application was intense, so the call from AFPC was met with mixed emotions. But who was I to argue with the Air Force? If I genuinely believed humility was a true sign of strength, this was a prime opportunity to apply the principle.

THE SCREAMING DEMON

The 2004 CFD started the same day as space and missile school graduation. It would be my third consecutive year fighting bulls at Cheyenne. Representing the USAF in the arena was my additional duty: my marketing mission. Just like the NASCAR No. 21 did on the track and Thunderbirds did in the air, I, too, promoted the brand to a specific demographic.

While away at school, CFD made a few key personnel adjustments. Long-time CFD bullfighters Rick Chatman and Dwayne Hargo retired and based on tenure, I was elevated to senior bullfighter.

Rick had been the senior bullfighter for the majority of his 19 years at CFD. Now it was my task to help the next generation settle into the rhythm of CFD.

Frontier Days is unlike most rodeos. Every hour brings unique obligations. From media interviews, to flipping pancakes, to autograph sessions, to parades, each day has its own full agenda. Some cowboys enjoy promoting events; others despise it.

Mike Matt was one of the fighters who earned a spot on the new roster.

All of this was exciting, but I faced one huge predicament: *How I could get from graduation in California to the rodeo in Cheyenne on the same day?*

Just like my original assignment to F.E. Warren, God had already prepared a way. The school's commandant concluded it was in the best interest of the Air Force that I miss graduation and head to Cheyenne.

Only 24 hours and 1,250 miles stood in between me and the "Daddy of 'Em All." Traveling by way of a 1978 Mercedes Benz 300D—top speed, 65 miles per hour—a photo finish was in my future.

I lovingly called the car the "Screaming Demon"—an interesting name for a car that couldn't be pulled over for speeding on the interstate. Actually, the name had little to do with speed and everything to do with a horrible belt noise. Whenever the air conditioner was on, this little green beauty would indeed scream.

Ira McKillip, my good friend and frequent traveling partner, flew to California to help me drive. Ira was a character, a real life modern-day drifter. Traveling the world was one of his biggest pleasures. Helping a friend in this case was merely a byproduct!

Kriszti stayed behind to tour California, so Ira and I had roughly 24 hours in the screaming demon to talk rodeo, life, career, and a multitude of other selfish ambitions. When we arrived in Cheyenne, I had basically edged God out of my mind. My confidence had clearly spilled over into dangerous territory.

We rolled into town with two hours to spare—just enough time to shake off the where-we-came-from dust.

BLINDED BY LIMELIGHT

God had given me an opportunity that only He could arrange, and more than once, I forgot that truth. The limelight suggested the great things He was doing in my life were by my design.

What a missed opportunity on my part.

God put numerous people in my path the following nine days. Likely, some needed to hear of Christ's love. Instead, they got stories about a small-town kid protecting freedom by day and cowboys by night.

The environment surrounding rodeo is just like any occupation or sport with a following. Although rodeo doesn't have the same scale audience, there is still sex, drugs, and rock-n-roll.

It doesn't take long in a circus to get distracted.

I was caught by the glitz and glamour and oblivious to what God was trying to do through me.

Around day four, rain started to pour day and night. The arena was a sloppy mess. Yet the show and party went on. Fighting bulls in ankle-deep mud, covered with shin-high water added another element of danger to the sport. The treacherous conditions coupled with mean 1,800-pound bulls—not to mention my current state of mind—all worked together to teach me a powerful lesson.

That afternoon I was caught show boating, and a bull hooked me in my right hamstring. The impact launched me seven feet straight up. From the aerial view, the bull's horns looked more like Louisville Slugger baseball bats!

When my feet finally returned to earth, he plowed me like garden soil, mauling me across the back. As the angry beast ran over me, he smashed every inch of my six-foot, three-inch frame into the mud.

"What in the world just happened?" I asked Mike as he laughed uncontrollably.

I wasn't hurt badly, a few cuts and scrapes, but my pride was busted. Sure, it's a bullfighter's job to take a "hooking" to keep a rider safe, but this "hooking" was a direct result of seeking the spotlight.

Show boating a touchdown celebration is pretty safe in comparison. A big linebacker isn't going to blitz and tackle an overzealous end-zone dancer! Rodeo is different. There are no referees, timeouts, or helmets. And bulls don't stop when the eight-second whistle blows.

Two days later, another bull managed to kick me square in the face. This time, it was at least in attempt to protect a fallen rider, not show boating. Nonetheless, it provided a painful reminder that I wasn't in charge. This bull flipped me backward and rendered me unconscious. As a parting gift, I awoke with a grade three concussion, a black eye, and what the doctors diagnosed as a traumatic brain injury.

Here's the thing about cowboys and cowgirls—we learn to play with pain. Most cowboys carry a tube of "Suck-it-Up" in their gear bag at all times. You can rub the cream on any bump, bruise, sprain, break, or even bad attitude. It works instantaneously!

When I came to, I asked the doctor to rub 12 ounces of "Suck-it-Up" on my head as I recited Philippians 4:13.

Being kicked in the face by a bull could have killed me, but, as Mom always said, "God takes care of fools and babies." I was a 27-year-old man who was often making foolish choices. Good thing God doesn't take days off.

Maybe rodeo is God's humorous way of humbling rough and

tough cowboys. Bulls don't read résumés, and they don't care if you're a world champion, a rookie, or somewhere in between.

It doesn't matter to God either. According to James 4:6, "God opposes the proud but shows favor to the humble." (ESV)

Beaten and battered after a long nine days, I learned that the hard way. It is God who gives, and it is God who takes away. For He can accomplish His plan with or without us.

COWBOY LOGIC

1. Describe a time when God worked for your good and His glory.

2. How has pride diverted your attention off of the Giver to the gift?

3. Outline a divine sequence of events that God inspired in your life.

...With man this is impossible, but for God everything is possible.

Matthew 19:26 (ESV)

chapter 7
A SHAKY START

Principle No. 6: Cowboy Up—Know Your Priorities

You might have noticed that the previous chapter began with the story of my marriage and then said very little about it once Kriszti and I moved to Wyoming. Other than moving to California together for my space and missile training, we both began blazing trails independent of each other.

We were young and eager to pursue our personal dreams, but we were blind to the fact our marriage was off to a shaky start. She spent most of her days working toward a career in basketball. And I, of course, focused my every moment on bullfighting goals and my Air Force career.

Kriszti and her family struggled from the start to understand my love for rodeo.

In Hungary, as in most of Europe, rodeo is a foreign concept. The Olympics serve as their benchmark for athletic success. In the United States, basketball players dream of playing in the NBA, football players dream of playing in the NFL, baseball players want to make it to the Major Leagues, and rodeo cowboys dream of making it in the PRCA.

Kriszti and her family, however, could not fathom why a person would participate in such a dangerous activity. They were flabbergasted that America even considered rodeo a sport.

Their disregard for rodeo pushed me even more.

By 2005, our selfish choices—often disguised as determination—were catching up to us. My determination had helped me overcome electrocution, finish college, earn my ProRodeo card, and survive the Air Force's Officer Training School. But sometimes my determination took me down the wrong path or cost me more than I should have paid.

Those hard lessons caused me to re-align my priorities during my journey and adopt the Cowboy Up principle. It's a simple principle about aligning priorities so that you can give a task everything you have, even if the odds are stacked against you. The principle reminds me that determination is a daily choice that has to be made with your priorities in the right order.

Tuff Hedeman made the "Cowboy Up" phrase famous in the movie *8 Seconds*. He motivated his friend, world champion bull rider Lane Frost, with the phrase by suggesting Frost could mentally block out pain, overcome an injury, and simply focus on riding the next bull.

While I had been spared major injuries, I wasn't free from pain. Being hooked and gored paled in comparison to our struggling marriage.

The Cowboy Up principle told me to get my priorities in order and do the right things for the right reasons. Unfortunately, I often strayed from this principle and ended up working with great determination but was driven by misaligned priorities.

WORLDS APART

My brand as the United States Air Force's only professional bullfighter was established and opportunities were growing. The Air Force helped promote me the way sports agents promote their clients.

As my career gained speed, however, Kriszti's stalled. After college, she had turned down opportunities with the Women's National Basketball Association (WNBA) to focus on our marriage. While admirable, it was a decision she later would regret, as did I.

The thrill of basketball and the pursuit of her passion eventually took new life. She annually traveled to Hungary, training with the national team. And before long she was afforded the opportunity to compete in Hungary.

I supported her decision. Her hopes of representing Hungary were driving her. Who was I to stand in her way?

We managed to maintain a long-distance relationship while focusing on our individual careers. I recall telling the *Denver Post*, "When it is all said and done, we don't want to look back and say we could have done this or we could have done that."

Certainly there were extended periods when we were together in the United States, but even then, our focus wasn't always on each other. While she did love me, many nights Kriszti lay awake crying. She often felt *stuck* in a relationship and *stuck* in America.

We tried to make it work despite the early warning signs. But when she became pregnant, the signs became more obvious. Perhaps it was a combination of hormones and homesickness. Regardless, our foundation started to crack.

On May 30, 2005, we welcomed a son, Jas Kornél Sparks. For me, nothing in my life had equaled the overwhelming emotions that came with the birth of my son. The birth of Jas was, and forever will be, one of my best days. I had never been so proud!

With that pride came the realization that we needed to reevaluate our priorities. I began to think about what it meant to put "family first" and about the future we could have together.

The joy that greeted me in the delivery room, however, was overshadowed by cultural issues and communication barriers with Kriszti's family.

Her parents had traveled from Hungary to Wyoming to help us adjust to life with a newborn. Jas was their first grandchild. So they came prior to his arrival and planned to stay through the summer.

It was great to have help with the baby, but my father-in-law and I were often at odds. Prior conversations regarding my "stupidity for being a rodeo cowboy" had never set well with me. I remained on the defensive. Plus, I felt he saw himself as the alpha male. In his mind, he could call the shots for my family in my home, just as he did for his family in his home.

Our communication barrier added complexity to our relationship.

Whether he knew it or not, he was constantly driving a wedge between Kriszti and me. And on the day of Jas' birth, the wedge was hammered even deeper. As the nurse completed the routine checks and swaddled Jas in a soft, blue blanket, she turned and handed me my son.

How awesome! I thought.

Quite naturally, I said in a baby voice as if he could understand, "I've got to get you in your momma's hands." I knew she was just as excited to experience unconditional love.

As I handed Jas to his mother, however, I heard my father-in-law from the corner of the room, speaking passionately in their native tongue.

You read that right. Her parents were in the delivery room immediately following his birth. I felt it was just another show of force on her dad's part. To me, it seemed a little premature.

My in-laws didn't speak any English, and I didn't speak any Hungarian. I had no idea what her father was saying, but I had some experience interpreting their tone and non-verbal cues. I could see the frustration in his face and hear it in his voice. So I suspected he wasn't making a hospital-wide endorsement of my merits as a husband and father.

"What is your dad saying, and why does he seem to be upset?" I asked Kriszti.

She didn't feel like translating, and how could I blame her—she had just given birth. I regretted even asking what was going on. But clearly her dad had something to say.

Furthermore, she was a little put out with me. Her doctor was a rodeo fan and wanted to talk shop while she was trying to focus on breathing and pushing! I totally missed picking up on her frustrations and fielded the typical fan's questions: "How bad have you been hurt?" and so on and so forth.

Nonetheless, it turns out, her dad felt I had lessened his experience as a first-time grandparent. Go figure!

The thought of setting aside my ambitions to submit to his dominance evaporated that very moment.

Kriszti was in an awkward situation. It was shaping up to be a choice between her husband and her family. I sincerely hated to see her in that predicament. I loved my parents dearly and certainly wouldn't have appreciated them coming between us in a similar way.

This was a choice she would have to make.

We knew that Matthew 19:5 taught, "For this reason a man will leave his father and mother and be united to his wife, and the two will become one flesh." (NIV) Like most truths, however, the application can be difficult. It was especially difficult when blending nationalities and theologies.

THE HUNGARIAN WAY

Despite the unfortunate turn of events, leaving the hospital with a healthy baby was a true blessing. Returning home knowing that the in-laws were going to be staying? Not so much!

Everyone was ecstatic to bring Jas home. Kriszti was a first-time mom. I was a first-time dad. Her parents were first-time grandparents. We all had our ideas about caring for Jas, but there was one thing we all shared—a deep love for this baby.

It quickly became clear that I was fighting a losing battle. In their minds, the only suitable way to raise Jas was the Hungarian way.

To be around the baby, family and neighbors had to scrub down with hand sanitizer; this wasn't presented as a polite request, but as a pointed demand.

To hold him, he first had to be placed on a special Hungarian pillow; without it, his back wouldn't develop straight.

When bathing him, only Hungarian soaps and creams could be used; without it, his skin would not be soft and smooth.

None of those things were horrible, of course. Frankly, I hoped our son would appreciate his heritage—the Hungarian and the cowboy. But I often felt like an outsider in my own home. My opinions and desires were often belittled and devalued. It appeared as if they were smart; I was stupid. They were right; I was wrong. I didn't feel invisible, but something worse. I felt like I was an irritation they were forced to live with.

Their attempts to ingrain the Hungarian culture were relentless, and there was no reason for me to question their ways. As they put it, "You have never been a dad before, so you don't know."

It was baffling for me to understand why Kriszti wouldn't stand up for our little family. I guess as I looked to rodeo for my future, she looked to her parents for hers. Nonetheless, I was puzzled by their culture and my father-in-law's overwhelming influence on my wife.

Watching these events unfold should have required me to Cowboy Up like never before.

When comedian Ron White tells his "Tater Salad" story about

being arrested, he points out he had the right to remain silent…he just didn't have the ability. That was my case, as well. I had the right to Cowboy Up, just not the ability. I didn't know what to do or how to stand up for what was rightfully mine.

BULLS, BRONCS, AND BARRELS

Four days after Jas came home, I received a call from Mike Matt.

"Sparks, I'm running late getting to the College Finals," he said. "Can you fill in for me at the Bulls, Broncs, and Barrels deal?"

The College National Finals Rodeo (CNFR) is known as the Rose Bowl of rodeo. It is an awesome event held in Casper, Wyoming inside a coliseum that seats 8,000 people. But more important than performing at a good rodeo was the opportunity to help Mike—the guy who'd helped me so much over the years.

My only dilemma—and it was a big one—was leaving Jas. He was one week old. While I sought opportunities to get out of the house, I wasn't eager to leave him, even if it was only for a couple of days. Not even one week into fatherhood, and already I was faced with choosing between family and rodeo.

Surprisingly, Kriszti supported my desire to choose rodeo. She was in good company. Her parents weren't leaving any time soon. It seemed like a win-win situation! I would be out of the house, away from her dad, and at a rodeo to boot.

So I packed my gear bag and headed to Casper, leaving Jas and his mom behind. I took just enough clothes for a two-day trip—the jeans around my waist and the shirt on my back.

The commissioner of the National Intercollege Rodeo Association was John Smith—the same John Smith who had been the rodeo coach at McNeese State University back in 1995. And after the

Sunday performance, he called me to the side to talk. But it wasn't to catch up on how life was treating his former recruit.

"Where is Mike Matt?" he asked bluntly.

"Mr. John," I said, "he called me saying he was running late."

He proceeded, still in a matter-of-fact tone.

"When will he be here?"

I didn't know, so I stepped aside and dialed Mike.

"Mike," I said with a sense of urgency, "you need to call Mr. John right now!"

Mr. John had a rodeo to produce, sponsors to satisfy, spectators to entertain, and a business to run. He counted on people being in place, on time, and ready to go. The production aspect of the College National Finals Rodeo in Casper is on par with the National Finals Rodeo in Las Vegas, using many of the same personnel. It is high-pressure and high-visibility with ESPNU documenting every ride.

Mr. John couldn't afford to leave any aspect of the event unbuttoned. He certainly didn't need the added burden of micromanaging contracted performers.

I'm not sure how the entire conversation between Mike and Mr. John went down, but I did hear Mr. John's end of the call. It wasn't pleasant.

I almost fainted. I was in shock for Mike because the CNFR was too good of a rodeo to lose. Furthermore, he had been a staple at the event since our 1999 summer campaign.

I also feared Mike would think that I had somehow undercut him. Rodeo could be a dirty business. I took great pride in never stooping to the levels that I saw as the norm. In a dog-eat-dog, back-stabbing business, my brand as a straight-shooter and man of principle was far more important than contracting with a good rodeo.

In interview after interview, I always made a point to say it was more important to be known as a good person than a good bullfighter. Even though I struggled at times, I knew the day would come when I would no longer be known by my athletic abilities. But there will never be a day that I won't be identified or known by my character.

This notion had been tested a year prior when the Pendleton Round-up was looking to make a change to their bullfighter personnel. Loyd Ketchum, as I mentioned, was a legend in the sport, but they were looking for a change by adding young talent. I was on the short list of guys they were considering.

The committee invited me out to meet the board members, socialize, and enjoy their rodeo. While flattered, making the trip wasn't my style, so I declined the offer. I respected Loyd as bullfighter and the business too much to fly to Oregon and circle around like a vulture, waiting to devour his job. Although business is business, integrity is priceless.

The CNFR situation was no different. It wasn't worth losing a friend or my integrity.

When Mr. John and Mike ended their call, Mr. John asked me to step inside the CNFR command center—a hotel suite that had been converted into a makeshift conference room for the rodeo's high brass. I would have rather walked into a four-star general's office. My back was straight and my posture rigid. It was definitely military mode.

Given the circumstances, I was slightly uncomfortable being in the presence of the who's who of rodeo production. These were the exact people who produced the National Finals. Their focus was more on the ends than the means.

I could sense the frustration and tension among the staff. To my surprise, however, they were welcoming, even elated to speak with me. Mr. John announced that there was an immediate need for a CNFR bullfighter. On the spot, I was hired for the job.

It was a moment of mixed emotions. While it was great to be deemed worthy to perform at such a prestigious event, it was equally heartbreaking knowing what had just transpired. My main concern was not losing a friendship over a rodeo. In fact, it strained our relationship, but, as real friends do, we eventually worked through it.

In a matter of hours, my two-day, one-night trip was extended to eight days and seven nights. My wardrobe remained the clothes on my back!

Despite Kriszti's and my differences, our mentality was similar when it came to goals. We agreed that, one day, opportunities would come. Success would follow hard work and determination.

Being so determined to help Mike and showcase my talents, I totally missed the mark of what should have been a higher priority. Leaving Jas and failing to lead my new family was a prime example of getting my own principle backward.

LIFE IN A KALEIDOSCOPE

Every opportunity couldn't be a No. 1 priority, but it was difficult for me to say no. Much like dropping everything to help Mike, that was my mindset in most facets of life.

I took a lot of pride in my determination.

To rodeo committees, event producers, sponsors, and the like, it was a quality they highly valued. My personal brand was trust. Furthermore, I genuinely liked going the extra mile.

Roughly 30 days later, Mike and I were back together, working Cheyenne. It was my fourth and his second year. At a big rodeo like the "Daddy of 'Em All," a typical day consisted of waking up at 4 a.m. to make a live morning news interview, only to rush back to a parade or public relations opportunity, then prepare for the rodeo and fight 40-60 bulls. When the rodeo was over, it was typical to engage fans for an hour, take more media interviews, and finally clean up from battling the bulls.

But the night was just beginning.

After cleaning up, supper was rushed because other engagements and promotional events were scheduled. And, of course, I typically wanted to save a little time to enjoy the perks that came with the job—access to the concerts, sponsors, and beer gardens.

It was common to field 50 interview requests and amass 100 hours promoting the event. That didn't include the actual time spent fighting bulls.

It was an honor to promote CFD, the CNFR, and every rodeo I worked. I wouldn't have had it any other way. That's who I was. But my determination to rodeo came at a price.

In an effort to establish parameters, hoping to level what was an already slippery slope, I had to manage my life better.

Mom taught my brothers and me from day one what the order of our priorities should be: God first, others second, self last. It sounded good.

When I pledged Pi Kappa Alpha back at UCA, the fraternity taught us what our priorities should be: God, family, school, and fraternity. It looked good on paper. In reality, fraternity and school ran first and second. Time for God and family was often hard to come by.

My priorities were constantly shifting and typically out of balance.

While striving to reach new heights, the struggle to discern what was for my good and His glory became increasingly difficult. Setting and applying guardrails never seemed as simple as Mom or the fraternity suggested.

For me, the idea of balancing life's priorities is more like a kaleidoscope than a scale. There are many random shapes and colors in life—priorities, if you will. In my case, it included God, family, the Air Force, rodeo, friends, volunteer work, and hobbies. The kaleidoscope tube represents a person's life, and the end cap that turns to make the picture represents God.

As you know, there is no easy way to remove a particle from the kaleidoscope without damaging the tube or its contents.

When I have trusted God to determine my priorities, everything has lined up and come into beautiful focus. But when I have been determined to line up my life on my own, it has become a hodge-podge of random bits and pieces.

The kaleidoscope concept doesn't limit God to being "a priority" that could be segmented from other priorities. It allows me to see God as an integral piece of every aspect of my life. Together, all of the unique pieces of me have the potential to become that beautiful picture. But could I really discern my true priorities?

COWBOY LOGIC

1. List your top five priorities.

2. How much time is spent on each?

3. Now arrange your priorities based on the time devoted to each.

4. Are relationships being sacrificed in your life?

5. In what ways can you commit more time to your top priorities?

6. What examples come to mind when you have put more faith in your own abilities rather than in God's ability?

I am the vine; you are the branches. Whoever abides in me and I in him, he it is that bears much fruit, for apart from me you can do nothing.

John 15:5 (ESV)

chapter 8
THE FINE LINE

Principle No. 7: The Razor—Confidence is a Fine Line

Basketball and rodeo had steadily pulled our family apart. Add to that the in-law situation, and you had kerosene on a campfire.

While my in-laws' desire to be in Jas' life was innocent and understandable, I questioned their motives at times, especially as it became more and more obvious that they wanted Jas to be raised as a Hungarian.

It seemed as if pitting Kriszti and me against each other was fair game.

Verbal attacks were one tactic to get me off balance, and they became a frequent occurrence. Many times that summer my father-in-law would lash out at me with what translated to, "You are stupid." "You could never get a job in Hungary." "Rodeo is not a sport." "You are not a real athlete." Words can be more hurtful than we know, and they started to take their toll on me in more ways than I realized.

It was hard on Kriszti, too. She was forced to translate, often through tears. And whether she agreed with her dad or not, translating the confrontations was intense.

The most explosive confrontation occurred late one afternoon when I returned from military duty after pulling a 36-hour ICBM combat alert. It had been a long, stressful shift at the controls of the most powerful weapon system in the world. I was ready to be at home. Shave, shower, and sleep never sounded so good.

Walking in the house, I noticed a large pile of the in-laws clothes in the center of the living room floor. I laid down on the floor, near the pile, and began to play with Jas. Whispering to Kriszti, I said, "Tell your parents they are welcome to use our laundry room."

Where have they been doing their laundry all this time? I wondered.

"My dad put them there to teach you a lesson," she said.

I was confused.

"To teach me a lesson?" I replied.

She assured me that was correct.

"What kind of lesson is he hoping to teach me?" I asked.

Turns out, he didn't like me undressing in my bathroom and laying my clothes on the floor—in my home—the home I had bought without using one Hungarian forint to purchase. He preferred clothes be placed in the laundry hamper prior to bathing. In his world, clothes didn't go on the floor.

Another show of force.

As Kriszti translated the "lesson," the tension in our living room rocketed. Her mom was quietly sitting in the corner, gazing out of the large picture window.

I moved from playing with Jas on the floor to sitting next to Kriszti on the couch. She picked Jas up and held him close. I could feel her nervous energy.

Her dad paced back and forth in front of me like a caged lion, roaring in his native tongue.

Feeling threatened, I turned to Kriszti and, in a calm voice, gave her a message to translate.

"Tell your dad if he touches me, I will knock him through that picture window."

Kriszti knew I wasn't kidding and that I was capable. While she had witnessed her dad get intense, this was by far the most bizzare she'd ever seen him. Nonetheless, she now had the duty to inform her dad in a language that he could understand.

When he heard her words, he sat down.

I have no idea what she translated, but without a doubt I had heard enough. His show of force was quickly moving to my application of power.

While that "lesson" ended, many tirades followed. And it was in his overconfidence to dominate our lives that I began to fully recognize the fine line between confidence and brass. It's a double-edged precept.

The Razor principle became a fitting way to help me regulate my mentality regarding confidence. I earned the call sign "Razor" as a student at the space and missile school. Bullfighting and my military career both called for confidence, but I also needed to realize that conceit would prohibit me from living out my calling. The line between the two can be razor thin, but I never wanted to cross into a position where my confidence degraded people.

INTO THE VALLEY

As summer came to its end, Kriszti received another invitation to train with the Hungarian national team. Age was catching up with her, and she feared this may be her last chance.

I was eager to have my family together without the in-laws around, but I supported her return to Hungary. She had supported my desire to fight bulls at the CNFR following Jas' birth, and I knew how much a shot at making the national team meant to her.

Shortly after her parents returned home, she left for Hungary. In her possession was a round-trip ticket and a quiet confidence that her basketball dreams were within reach. When the plane took off,

Jas was sitting on his mom's lap. He, too, would live in Hungary while she gave basketball one final sacrifice.

I remained in Wyoming. I had no idea what a mistake this would be.

I didn't see it then, but a master plan was falling into place. Taking Jas to Europe was the first move in establishing his Hungarian residency and another step toward ending our marriage.

Kriszti was supposed to know within a few months if she had made the team, but roughly three months later she said she needed to stay and keep practicing. She and Jas returned to Wyoming in 2006 for almost three months, but they went back to Hungary shortly after Jas turned one. Again, they left with a round-trip ticket, but this time they never returned.

In December, I went to Hungary, and it was obvious to both of us there was no hope for our marriage. I stayed a week, slept on the couch in her parents' home, and felt like the unwanted foreigner that I was. I made things worse by losing my cool and lashing out with unkind words that I later regretted.

By now, Kriszti and I were living completely different lives, separated by geography and emotionally detached. In my mind, she moved on, choosing basketball and Hungary. In her mind, I moved on, choosing rodeo and America. With time, we'd both accept more personal responsibility for our mistakes in the marriage. But in the moment, we each were quick to place all the blame on the other. I guess she thought if I loved her, I would have traveled to Hungary and fought for her to return. I know I thought if she loved me, she wouldn't have left in the first place.

Regardless of who we felt was right and who we felt was wrong, the result was divorce.

One hot afternoon, my doorbell rang, and a fellow stood with a large envelope in hand, peeping through my screen door.

"Sir, how can I help you?" I said.

"Are you Jeremy Sparks?" he asked.

"Yes."

"I have some papers for you."

"What kind of papers?" I inquired.

"Something to do with child support," he replied.

"I don't pay child support," I told him matter-of-factly.

Without missing a beat he said, "Well, you are about to."

The papers he served, of course, were divorce and child custody documents. He was right. Child support was in my future.

I had no idea she had started the process, much less filed, but it certainly didn't come as a huge surprise. Divorce was inevitable and actually a welcomed relief. I knew for years that it was coming, and I had even talked once to a lawyer about it while Kristzi was away; I just didn't have it in me to file.

As I read the translated version of the case, I wasn't thinking about myself. I only worried for Jas and what was best for his future.

What in the world will become of my child?

The papers listed the reason for the divorce as, "My husband did not care about me, or Kornél, instead he has devoted himself to his hobbies."

Our marriage hadn't crumbled because of one person. It had failed in part because we were overconfident in our quest to pursue individual greatness while neglecting each other.

Shouldn't it have also mentioned that she chose basketball and her home country? I thought. *Or that her family wanted to raise my son a Hungarian?*

While divorce is atrocious, this case was unique because the Hungarian government made rulings in both our divorce and child custody cases. This left me at an obvious disadvantage when it came to fighting for my parental rights.

By the day after I received the papers, our joint bank account had been emptied of all but $50.01. On top of that, Kriszti was seeking what I felt was an excessive amount for alimony and child support. And, worst of all, she was asking for significant restrictions on my visitation rights—a brief window each summer in which I could see my son for one week and only while supervised by Kriszti until he turned three.

I spoke zero Hungarian and felt sure it would be a disaster if I showed up for a court hearing there, especially without legal assistance. I talked to several attorneys—from Cheyenne to New York City—but none who could help. A few expressed empathy, but said they lacked the expertise to fight in an international court.

So with me in Wyoming feeling helpless and in more pain than any bull had ever inflicted, the Hungarian court granted Kriszti everything she had requested.

There was little choice other than to accept the Hungarian ruling. In total, I invested nearly $10,000 in legal fees only to be told it would take more research, more lawyers, and more money—all with little hope for what I ultimately wanted, which was to lower the financial burden and, most of all, to spend more time with Jas.

For the first time in my life, I had zero desire to fight. So I surrendered, agreeing to pay the alimony and child support mandated by the courts—$16,800 in alimony and child support for the first six months, $33,120 over the next 18 months, and $11,000 a year after that until Jas turned 18. With the stroke of my signature, agreeing to those conditions, Kriszti vaulted up her countries' social status ladder. On a positive note, Jas would be provided for.

Hungarian certified documents arrived every week. I was put out and found each one more difficult than the last. But one document was particularly heartbreaking. After our divorce was settled, I was notified that Kriszti had petitioned the court to have Jas' name changed—his *first* name!

The name Jas came from my initials—Jeremy A. Sparks. From the time I was old enough to even think about having kids, I knew this was to be my first son's name. Kriszti knew this, too, long before we married, and obviously she agreed on May 30, 2005.

She proposed his new name be Sparks-Hollósy Kornél. "Jas is no Hungarian name," she added. In all fairness, she had discussed changing his name since taking him back to Hungary.

Nonetheless, when I read the document, I was hurt. She had already taken my son from me. She had already restricted our future visits. Now she wanted to change his name.

The document called for my signature, although I was sure it was only a formality, not a point for contention or consideration. I didn't like seeing Jas used as a pawn, so reluctantly I signed the paper. His mom and I had created this mess, and I wanted to shield him when possible. Even if it meant changing his name, I wouldn't retaliate.

MY GOOD SAMARITAN

After selling the house, I moved to the campground on F.E. Warren Air Force Base. My new abode was a 19-foot travel trailer that I often pulled to circuit rodeos.

Missing out on most of the "firsts" that come with a newborn and being a new dad stirred up a lot of emotions. Sitting around a campfire was the perfect setting to reminisce and doctor the pain.

At times, it was almost too much to bear.

On one hand I was bitter, hurt, broken, sad, and mad. On the other hand, I was relieved and excited. Faced with the decision to either fall into depression or recommit to living my dream, I had to choose.

How could I find the confidence to regain my will to fight? I wondered.

Verl and Mary Smedley, who lived next door to the home Kriszti and I owned, had been good to us since the day we bought the house. Smed, as I called him, was a World War II veteran and an old cowboy. Ms. Mary was a retired nurse and devoted Christian—a saint in her own right.

Smed's grandmother was a Sparks. He knew we had to be kin.

"There just aren't too many Sparks," he would say.

Just like Donny and I bonded over our last name in 1991, Smed and I did the same.

Smed shared old-timer stories in an attempt to reduce the focus of my current situation. He understood that worry robbed happiness, and that kind words can cheer a heart (Proverbs 12:25).

It was clear to him that I was slipping. I constantly questioned myself about what I could have done differently, how I could have fought harder for my son. My heartbreak was palpable.

As Wyoming's winter set in, the camper was no longer a safe home. Pressured with love, the Smedleys insisted that I move in with them. I finally agreed.

While I was extremely grateful, it was a pretty humbling event.

They showed me an amazing testimony of God's love. Much like the Good Samaritan story in Luke, Chapter 10, I was knocked down, robbed, and wrecked. Ms. Mary and Smed picked me up from life's beating, took me in, cared for me, and treated me like a neighbor, the way God designed.

Smed's young adulthood was complicated. In many ways, he saw himself in me. He was a cowboy and a sailor. He had suffered through a bitter divorce, and experienced a gut-wrenching child custody case himself. His wisdom was profound and helped me rise out of the ashes.

Every day he would tell me to "lean forward," and assured me that, "It was a beautiful life, if I never weakened and gave up."

During my time of desperation, I often felt the closest to God. Maybe it was because everything had been stripped from me and there was nothing else to cling to.

Shortly after midnight one morning, I began to weep while praying. In the basement of the Smedleys' home, the Holy Spirit began to speak to me. For some reason, God was telling me to go to the First Baptist Church in Cheyenne and pray with the pastor (and friend), Jason King.

I knew it was God's voice, yet I tried to reason with Him.

"God, you know it is after midnight."

Still, I felt compelled to obey.

Around 1 a.m., I surrendered and drove to the church. As God would have it, Jason was walking out of the church as I turned onto the parking lot. I reached out for him with tears running down my face.

"Jason, God told me I would find you here," I said. "I need you to pray for me."

Even at my lowest, God was with me.

He used the Smeds, military buddy Kal Robinson, good friend France Clark, and my preacher to help me regroup and refocus. I spent many long hours with them, talking through life's challenges. And, of course, my parents and brothers supported me every step along the way. The desire to rodeo and my newfound confidence to never weaken helped fill the void of missing Jas.

During this time, many people in rodeo circles viewed me as a guy who'd been privileged to travel the world and work some of the best rodeos in the country. On the outside, I was a bright star in the midnight sky. A captain in the Air Force by day and a professional bullfighter by night.

On the inside, I fought a daily battle to lean forward.

But I couldn't let a setback, even a major one, derail my God-given dream.

SIGNS OF STRENGTH

The large majority of high performers I served with in the military and in sports had one common trait: confidence. How they handled their confidence and the source of their confidence, however, varied greatly.

Confidence is not a negative character quality. In fact, I pray my kids grow up to be confident in their faith, careers, family, and activities. I believe that confidence turns negative—dangerous—however, when its source is anything other than Christ.

My favorite verse is Philippians 4:13, when Paul proclaims, "I can do all things through Him who strengthens me." (ESV) The anchor of his profession was not in his ability, but in his Savior's ability.

In the valley of divorce and losing Jas, there was no question where my strength came from or who was responsible for my life. When required, God humbled me, making it painfully clear that He wanted all of the glory for my life.

There is a distinct line between confidence and conceit, confidence and arrogance, confidence and ego, and confidence and pride. Too often, I crossed over from confidence in my God-given abilities to selfish arrogance.

Pride was a pitfall I should have expected. The flesh has the ability to believe that we did it all, did it alone, and did it the best. In truth, the only thing that happens when pride moves in is that we move God out.

I knew that humility was a true sign of strength (Principle 5). But had I been living it consistently? When the scabs were peeled off, I had to get real with myself. Had my ego edged God out? Fooling people was easy. Fooling God, impossible.

He already knew.

According to scripture, and validated in my life, humility is a choice. Either I could humble myself and be lifted up, or remain in pride and be humiliated (Matthew 23:12).

Too bad I didn't pass Humility 101 the first time.

FINDING MY IDENTITY

Professional rodeo is broken into 12 geographic circuits, sort of like conferences in other sports. At the end of each season, the circuit bull riders vote for the top bullfighters. The two bullfighters who receive the most votes serve as the bullfighters during the annual circuit finals rodeo.

Working a circuit finals is pretty prestigious. Of all of the 150 eligible bullfighters in ProRodeo, only 24, two per circuit, earn the honor.

In the rodeo world, cowboys strive to win championships—a world title, national title, circuit title, or some other major rodeo title.

Since bullfighting no longer had a world championship, I thought being selected for a circuit finals would validate my career and provide a measure of identity. In 2004, and again in 2005, I received the third most votes in my circuit. I was the first loser.

I was in a vicious cycle chasing artificial fulfillment.

Time and time again, I saw friends and peers spend their lives pursing a title—sacrificing everything only to come up short of accomplishing their self-imposed goals. And every time, an empty void was exposed.

On the flip side, I witnessed world champions and accomplished individuals have their identity so tied to a title or accolade that without it they were empty shells, aimlessly searching for real peace.

At times, I was just as guilty.

It's not surprising that God required me to become more spiritually mature before freeing me to experience Jabez-sized blessings (1 Chronicles 4:10). It had nothing to do with my ability. It had everything to do with understanding the real source of my identity.

I had to realize it was all about Jesus and not at all about Jeremy.

Maybe I was a slow learner. It took a divorce, losing Jas, and falling short of my goals to expose my overconfidence and to begin addressing it in more positive ways.

LONG LIVE COWBOYS

I grew up admiring the endorsed rodeo athletes associated with major brands. Loyd Ketchum was the face of Bailey Hats, and I cherished my hand-me-down straw hat from Uncle Jerry and Aunt Sharon. Charlie Sampson, Ty Murray, Jake Barnes, Clay O'Brien Cooper, and, of course, Donny and Ronny were just a few top cowboys who represented Wrangler during my youth.

As a kid, I aspired to be a Wrangler Cowboy.

The company was the face of the Wrangler Bullfighting Tour. It had a long history of sponsoring only the best cowboys dating back to the Jim Shoulders era of the 1950s. Only a select few had the athletic abilities and character qualities that were in line with Wrangler's core values. Wearing Wrangler brought instant credibility. Even people outside of rodeo knew that a cowboy wearing the Wrangler brand bore the mark of a champion.

I tried for years to get my promotional packet on the desk of a Wrangler executive. I had a solid human interest story. The nation was at the height of patriotic flare, and I was a staple at Cheyenne Frontier Days.

Surely, my packet can get pushed forward, I thought.

Mike Matt, a three-time world champion, couldn't manage to strike a deal either. If any bullfighter could land a Wrangler deal, it should have been Mike. Wrangler sponsored three bullfighters at the time, and apparently they weren't looking for Mike or me. Our packets appeared to find Wrangler File 13. Never once did I get a reply.

In January of 2006, however, God opened a door.

I was spending a weekend skiing at the annual Cowboy Downhill in Steamboat Springs, Colorado. I'd met up with Charlie Sampson, a good friend and world champion bull rider to fellowship and ski fresh powder. Charlie had long retired, but the rodeo icon continued to endorse Wrangler.

One evening after skiing, he and I were invited to dinner with Karl Stressman. Karl was the director of event marketing for Wrangler and was responsible for their sponsorship program, but I didn't know that when we sat down to break bread. I was simply enjoying a complimentary steak dinner with a good friend.

Karl, Charlie, and I all discussed our passions, careers, and aspirations. Karl knew I was the "Air Force cowboy," but he didn't "know" me.

When we finished dinner, he asked me to mail him my portfolio.

I assured him that I would. What I thought was, *I have sent it every year for four years now!* But my momma didn't raise a fool!

A few weeks later, a true highlight in my career was realized, when I signed on as a Wrangler endorsee.

I'm sure it looked like luck to those who didn't know my story. In fact, when I signed the contract, I hadn't even worked a circuit finals yet. There were certainly other guys who had more complete resumes.

So how did a young guy with limited experience and exposure land a multi-year deal to represent Wrangler, the face of professional rodeo?

It's simple.

It was a God-appointed opportunity that had nothing to do

with me or luck. As a matter of fact, I wasn't even supposed to be in Colorado Springs that weekend. Charlie had invited me to join him as he was nearing Steamboat's city limits. Cheyenne is three hours away. I was already late when he called!

Representing Wrangler brought instant credibility, additional opportunities, and, of course, new challenges that would require me to apply the Razor principle.

With increased exposure, so was the likelihood of crossing the line from confidence to pride. Rodeo isn't as mainstream as sports like basketball, baseball, or football, but the passion of our fan base has no equal. They get into the sport and its athletes, and their well-meaning cheers can puff up egos and draw you over the line to pride.

Riding the momentum, I picked up events as far away as California and ultimately was selected for the Mountain States Circuit Finals Rodeo that November. But it didn't validate my abilities. It was a great experience and certainly a goal achieved, but that's all. Just another rodeo in which I hoped people could see God's light shine.

It was all His doing.

I have to remind myself to guard my heart and fight the temptation to focus inward. Matthew 6:19 says, "Do not store up for yourselves treasures on earth, where moths and vermin destroy, and where thieves break in and steal." (NIV) Staring at a trophy case was satisfying, but pointless.

I challenged myself to become more Christ-centered—every day, every month, and every year—having confidence in God throughout the journey. It's way too easy to praise God on the mountaintop, curse Him in the valleys, and seek control when things aren't going according to plan.

Knowing your true source of strength gives confidence to walk the fine line.

I'm living proof.

COWBOY LOGIC

1. What actions do you take when you see a friend, neighbor, or stranger in need?

2. In what areas of your life has self-confidence crossed the line to pride, conceit, or arrogance?

3. What is at the center of your passion, dream, and life? Who gets the glory?

Great is the LORD and most worthy of praise; his greatness no one can fathom.

Psalm 29:1 (NIV)

Power Steering

Man-handling a bull away from a fallen rider at the
2008 First Frontier Circuit Finals Rodeo in Harrisburg, Pennsylvania.

Photo by Eva Scofield

SECTION THREE
Letting Go

chapter 9

MY NEW CALLING

Principle No. 8: The Gold Buckle—Integrity Can't Be Bought

Lane Frost became a professional bull rider right after graduating from high school, and he won a world championship in 1987 when he was 24.

That not only earned him a coveted gold buckle, but also the opportunity the next year to take part in the Challenge of Champions. This special exhibition event was an epic man-against-bull battle between two great champions—Lane versus the mighty Red Rock, the reigning Bucking Bull of the Year.

Red Rock had not been successfully ridden by a bull rider in 309 attempts, and Lane would get seven shots at becoming the first. He not only successfully rode Red Rock for the eight-second minimum, he did it in four of the seven matches.

Growney Brothers Rodeo Company owned Red Rock, and John Growney was proud of his prized bull. But he was equally impressed by Lane Frost. In fact, the two became close friends.

John respected Lane's skills as a rider—after all, it took a great champion to ride Red Rock. But more than that, John respected Lane as a person—who he was, what he stood for, how he lived his life.

Tragically, Lane's life was cut short on a rainy day in 1989 in an accident at Cheyenne Frontier Days. After a successful bull ride, he was hooked by the bull's horns as he tried to escape. He wasn't pierced, but his ribs were broken, and one of those broken ribs ended up fatally puncturing his heart and lungs.

But Lane's legacy is legend. Buildings are named after him. Awards are created in his honor. And movies tell his story (*8 Seconds* starring Luke Perry tells his life story and the documentary *The Challenge of Champions* is about his battle with Red Rock).

At least five songs pay tribute to Lane, including *The Dance* by Garth Brooks. He's in the ProRodeo Hall of Fame, the PBR Ring of Honor, the Cheyenne Frontier Days Hall of Fame, and the Texas Cowboy Hall Fame. And his photo is on the cover of *The Cowboy Bible: The Living New Testament*.

Lane was larger than life, inside the arena and out, and few people knew him better than John Growney.

I never met Lane, but one of the highlights of my career came the summer I got to spend some time with John in Santa Maria, California. As John and I visited, out of the blue he looked up at me and said, "You remind me more of Lane Frost than any other person I've met since."

I didn't look like Lane Frost. We were both lanky, but pictures prove Lane was far prettier than me. To John, however, my life was a similar example of a joyous life.

I can't imagine receiving a higher compliment, especially from John, than to be compared in any way to Lane Frost. And while I knew how unworthy I was of that comparison, I was thankful that after all the peaks and valleys I'd been through, someone actually saw joy—a little of God's light—shining through me.

THE GOD FACTOR

Lane Frost had what many people call the "it factor"—that *something* you can't define, but you know when you see it.

I learned the term when I was selected for *The Power of 10,* a TV game show starring Drew Carey. The casting director contacted me after seeing my appearance on *Pressure Cook* with Chef Ralph Pagano.

"Jeremy, there is just something about you," the director said. "We'd love to fly you to New York City and have you on the show."

The casting director may have thought I had the "it factor." But like Lane Frost, the "it" he saw really had nothing to do with me. Rather, everything to do with what I prefer to call the "God factor." Galatians 5:22-23 describes the "God factor" as fruits of the Spirit: love, joy, peace, kindness, faithfulness, humility, and self-control. As my Grandmother Sparks would say, "Every Christian has a serious heart condition: it's called happiness!"

When those traits are on display, a life is marked by integrity that can't be bought and a light that shines so brightly that others can't help but take notice.

That light hasn't always shown brightly in my life. In truth, there were times I wondered if my light was still shining at all, especially knowing how divorce had impacted me.

Alimony and child support provided a monthly reminder that divorce sucks. Sending a hefty check to the ex-wife was difficult; sending it with a joyful heart was impossible.

I had learned a few lessons, however, and they would serve me well in the post-divorce stage of my journey.

One of them was Principle No. 8: The Gold Buckle—Integrity Can't Be Bought.

I had seen, both from my mistakes and from witnessing the

destructive behaviors of others, that our selfish desires are never more valuable than our personal integrity. And as I prioritized my integrity over my selfish desires, God helped me rise from the ashes of divorce, rebuild my life, and more consistently let His light shine through me.

NEW TRACTION

Rodeo continued to be my outlet. I was coming into my own as a bullfighter. Opportunities surged. New sponsors, new rodeos, new marketing deals, television commercials, and more reality TV.

During this time, Wyoming became the first state to use rodeo athletes to market their brand by featuring professional cowboys to promote travel and tourism to the Cowboy State. It was an exclusive sponsorship with excellent financial and fringe benefits.

To become an endorsee, you had to be a state resident and you had to qualify for the National Finals Rodeo. Although still stationed at F.E. Warren, I had not qualified for the National Finals, but the governor and executive council offered me the same sponsorship. I was the first, and at the time, the only bullfighter featured.

Before the ink dried on that deal, Bresnan Communication, a telecommunications company that, at the time, had more than 300,000 cable subscribers in Montana, Wyoming, Utah, and Colorado, selected me as the face of its brand. The tagline was, "Bresnan Territory: *Out Here, It's Personal.*"

Life-sized cutouts of me (dressed in full gear) were in every corporate and regional office. Plastered on billboards across the West was yours truly, standing stoic with a caption that read, "At least football players get to wear helmets." Commercials showing how I used a Bresnan DVR to study bull riding ran day and night in their target markets.

I traveled in a Dodge Ram 2500 Megacab 4x4 pickup that was paid for by a sponsor and wrapped like a NASCAR. My attire was similar: Sponsor logos covered almost every visible square inch. A logo on my sleeve went for $6,000. A logo on my back? $10,000-$15,000. Want front-and-center placement? Well, that was reserved for the Air Force. And I typically could negotiate a respectable $750 to $1,000 day rate—$5,000 for international exhibitions.

There were plenty of cowboy stars who made much more money than I did, but the days of earning $200 to $300 per performance and covering my own expenses were long gone.

As my name recognition grew, more senior leaders in the military took an interest and supported my career. From the Secretary of the Air Force to my wing commander, when the top brass was in town, my phone rang.

One year, Gen. Michael Moseley, the 18th Chief of Staff of the Air Force, was the Grand Marshall at Cheyenne Frontier Days. He spotted me getting ready to perform and made his way over.

"Jeremy, you bring great credit to the Air Force," he said as he stuck his hand out to greet me.

I was a little uneasy having the most senior Air Force officer on site to watch me perform. After all, I was government property and injury was always a concern.

"Sir, my pleasure meeting you," I said. "So I have your permission to proceed with the event today!"

God had delivered me from my messy situations, and one thing became clear—my mess had become my message. My test had become my testimony. All of this good fortune, however, came with unique challenges.

First, while it was a blessing to increase revenue, recognition, and expand my platform, the "razor" again was exposed. So I had to battle the temptations that came with walking the fine line between confidence and conceit.

Second, my success wasn't always well-received by others. Professional envy, both in the military and in rodeo, occasionally reared its ugly head.

More than anything, the devil desires to stop God's people from fulfilling their purpose in life. John 10:10 says, "The thief comes only to steal and kill and destroy." (ESV) That thief—the devil—comes in many shapes and sizes, and he even lurks in the military ranks and in the rodeo business.

God had opened so many doors. Sponsorships and public appearances generated more income than actually fighting bulls, and some of my rodeo peers didn't appreciate my marketability. Working the National Finals was never my goal. Being an officer limited my schedule to an extent; so the NFR was unrealistic. However, peers were perplexed that I could balance two careers. It frustrated some to see me book good rodeos and sign major endorsements while working a limited schedule.

Clearly, some valued the gold buckle of fame over integrity. And when they sold their integrity to advance their selfish goals at my expense, well, it put my Gold Buckle principle to the test.

MY BROKEN BUCKLE

One such test occurred in 2007 when I was selected to fight bulls at the Dodge National Circuit Finals Rodeo (DNCFR).

The event features the year-end and average champions from ProRodeo's 12 circuit finals. In other words, the top 24 contestants in each circuit finals rodeo face off in a unique winner-take-all, bracketed format.

A selection committee also picks two bullfighters and one alternate from the 24 who performed at the 12 circuit finals. So it's a high honor to get picked. Other than the National Finals Rodeo in Las Vegas, making the DNCFR is pretty prestigious. Obviously, I couldn't help but be excited—as were my friends, family, and sponsors.

When the news broke that December, buddies called to congratulate me. Family called for tickets. Random media outlets called to hear my story. CBS Morning News scheduled to be on hand to witness the Air Force bullfighter on the national stage. The PRCA's media department even called to interview me for a cover story in *The ProRodeo Sports News*. Its circulation is limited to rodeo fans, but it is "the" publication for all things ProRodeo.

Two months after I received the selection notification, however, the PRCA emailed me with some disheartening news: I had been bumped into the alternate bullfighter slot. Instead of being in the top two, I was the odd man out.

The event was scheduled to begin on March 14, so getting this news just a month prior was certainly frustrating. Perhaps a phone call would have been more appropriate.

The snafu occurred when the PRCA decided not to honor the committee's original vote count for what turned out to be political reasons.

When my identity was more closely aligned to a title, this might have been a devastating blow. As it was, I challenged the PRCA and many cowboys and circuit directors stood for me. But the leadership considered it a closed case. No new buckle for me.

Yes, it was hard to understand. Sure, I was disappointed. I even lost a little faith in mankind. Perhaps it simply wasn't God's will for my life. But one thing remained: My identity was in Christ, not as a bullfighter.

FINDING TRUE GOLD

Fighting the battles that come with life is never easy, but it's even harder to fight them without help from trusted friends.

God gave me many such friends in my journey. But in 2008, He blessed me with the best friend and helpmate I could ever imagine—a soulmate who would inspire me and encourage me to live the Gold Buckle principle and all the other principles in this book.

Our whirlwind romance actually went back nearly a decade.

In 1999, not long after I arrived at UAM, I left a note on a girl's Mustang. She was a senior and hard to miss—a blonde haired, brown-eyed beauty who was popular on campus. She had a sweet southern name, and it was printed on her license plate: JAMIEJO.

She also had a boyfriend and didn't like cowboys!

Those minor details didn't stop me from taking a shot, but I guess it missed the mark. I never heard from her. I doubt she even took the time to read the note. Most likely, she turned her windshield wipers on and let it fly away.

We became reacquainted through mutual friends after both of our first marriages fell apart. The moment I laid eyes on her all those years later, she was more beautiful and outgoing than I recalled. Her license plate no longer said JAMIEJO, but she was still just as easy to spot.

The very moment we reconnected, I knew that we would marry. (She holds fast to not having those feelings until a week later!) Early on in our relationship and before I had met her parents, I called her mom to introduce myself. When she picked up, I blurted out, "I'm Jeremy, your future son-in-law!"

"I think you're crazy!" she cackled.

I thought, *I'm just giving you fair warning.*

Jamie lived in Arkansas, and I was still stationed in Wyoming.

But with the help of airplanes and cell phones, we made the courtship work.

Coming out of divorce, we both knew what we were looking for in a mate. We shared the same beliefs, culture, values, and hopes for the future. In addition, her family quickly accepted me as their own. The thought of an extended family and in-laws embracing my rodeo career sealed the deal.

Jamie simply wanted to experience unconditional love and be treated with dignity and respect. My parents taught my brothers and me that we should love our wives as Jesus loved us. Dad tried his best to live the example he preached.

Granted, I failed miserably at loving my first wife unconditionally. However, I was committed to getting it right the next time. Divorce had pierced me too deep to get it wrong twice.

Jamie was the soulmate I needed as my spouse and life partner. She understood I was living my God-given dream, and I liked the thought of having a spouse who believed in me and in my calling. But I needed help with the details, and Jamie had a gift for the details.

Jamie quickly realized that I needed some parameters in my life. Without them, I was often off track. My brother Jeff told her prior to our wedding, "Whatever you do, don't dare him to do something." He had seen me march to my own beat my entire life. It was clear that everything that called my name wasn't for my good or God's glory. Yet that wasn't always enough to keep me grounded. For the first time in a long time, I had additional (and much needed) accountability in my life.

Jamie still wasn't fond of cowboys, but she loved *me*.

Standing at Gull Point on Lake Yellowstone inside the Yellowstone National Park, we said, "I do."

The ceremony was just what we were looking for: small, simple, and elegant. The weather was perfect with the bluest of skies. The scenery was certainly the best in the world, and we were surrounded by close friends and family. The original Yellowstone yellow bus carrying Jamie to the site made the perfect touch.

This was the first of many escapades we would enjoy together. We crisscrossed the entire country following Uncle Sam and the rodeo trail. Rodeo blessed us with unbelievable opportunities to witness, encourage, serve, and testify.

In our first year of marriage, we trekked from Santa Barbara, California to Harrisburg, Pennsylvania, making frequent stops along the way. We toured the wine country in California, hiked a 14,000-foot mountain in Colorado, climbed Wyoming's Devils Tower, went dog mushing in Jackson Hole, toured the Hershey Factory in Pennsylvania, and so much more.

As we traveled, my story continued to draw news media. The arrangement with the USAF continued, and I did a ton of public relations while bullfighting across the globe—somewhere around a hundred media engagements a year.

I was an officer first, but in the summer months I could string together a decent rodeo schedule. One summer in fact, I performed for 23 consecutive days from California to New York, facing more than 550 bulls. The winters and springs weren't nearly as busy, but the summers were always an adventure.

In Jeremiah 33, the word of God breathed, "Nevertheless, I will bring health and healing to it; I will heal my people and will let them enjoy abundant peace and security." Jamie and I were living this promise.

There weren't many rodeo goals left for me to accomplish. I had matured past selfish ambitions and the spotlight. Traveling, making memories, loving Jamie, and glorifying God were my main priorities.

Wherever we went, whatever we did, I wanted my heart content on being a vessel for God. By this time, I considered myself a stained glass window. God created a refreshing picture out of my brokenness for His light to shine. If the light was for a rodeo crowd or solely for Jamie, I was now content.

A HEAD STOMPING

While our wedding day was picture perfect, and the years that followed have been a blessed adventure, there was one aspect of our marriage that didn't start out so perfectly.

Ironically, it happened after God answered a prayer.

Deep down, I always wanted to work a professional rodeo with Donny before we both retired. He had been rodeoing 20-plus years, so time was running out. But we finally got the opportunity—two days after Jamie and I were married in Yellowstone.

While doing media engagements inside Yellowstone National Park on behalf of Wyoming Tourism, I developed a great love for this sublime park and the people who managed it. One of those people, Rick Hoeninghausen, grew up in New York but was always intrigued with the cowboy way of life. Sharing an interest in all things Yellowstone and cowboy, we fostered a great friendship.

Unbeknownst to me, Rick's good friend, Tim Mahieu, was on the rodeo committee for the Cody Stampede in Cody, Wyoming. He also was a fan of my work, having seen me perform at Cheyenne a few times. So when the Stampede decided to add fresh young blood to its bullfighting crew, my name was brought up.

In short, I was offered the job. And my partner at the event would be none other than Donny Sparks. He had been a staple at the Fourth of July event for 15 consecutive years. Now he would work it with his protégé, at his next to last rodeo of his legendary career!

Before the ink dried on my contract, you would have thought it had deflated bullfighters across the country—regardless of whether they had connections to the Stampede. In fact, a few despondent cowboys found enough political strings to pull behind the scenes that it created the DNCFR squabble all over again.

It was sad to see, but it reinforced my belief in the Gold Buckle principle. Integrity can't be bought. And if you have to sin to get something, it isn't a blessing.

Like signing with Wrangler, people who didn't really know me thought my selection at Cody was just another run of good luck. What they didn't know was that I had been praying since I was 14 for the opportunity to one day fight bulls with Donny. As minuscule a prayer it may seem, it was my heart's desire.

Everything in my career was made possible by following the Saint Augustine model: Working as if it depended on me and praying as if it depended on God. The Cody Stampede was no different.

God sent me to F.E. Warren in Cheyenne, and God redirected my assignment to keep me there. God opened the doors leading to Wyoming Tourism. God put Rick in my path. God put Tim in Rick's path. And God put Tim in a position to search for a bullfighter.

The result: 17-year-old prayer answered!

Jamie's family had flown out to Yellowstone for the wedding and extended their stay to watch the rodeo.

When that first night of rodeo was over, I could have quit bullfighting with no regrets. It was a great moment for both Donny and me, a highlight in my career—like a young basketball player finally getting to play an NBA game alongside Michael Jordan or LeBron James.

Although we were hired for cowboy protection, the rodeo producers arranged an exhibition freestyle bullfight. On the second night of the event, we partnered in razzling and dazzling a mean fighting bull.

Even at 43, Donny was still impressive. We danced with the wild beast for 60 seconds. It was a fearful yet exhilarating minute of my life. Saving his best trick for last, Donny started to put distance between himself and the bull. It was obvious he was setting up his signature move—jumping the bull from head to tail.

As Donny created the runway, the bull wouldn't fully commit to charging, making the jump nearly impossible. Out of concern I shouted, "Donny, what are you thinking?"

Just as I had taken his advice all of those years, he accepted mine in that moment. In a weird way, I was relieved that he didn't tempt fate. I thought, *I know you can jump the bull, but for what?* He didn't have anything to prove, and it wasn't worth him risking injury.

Plus, we still had 10 bull riders to protect.

One of those riders was matched against a big black bull with brimming horns. As the bull violently threw the cowboy to the ground, roughly three seconds into the ride, I "shot the gap" to save him.

While the fallen rider escaped unscathed, the bull drove a horn into my back, knocking me down. The protective vest, worn under my shirt, prevented a puncture wound. But I knew immediately that I was hurt. Scrambling to get up, both back hoofs came crashing down on my head, rendering me unresponsive.

Medics rushed to my aid, and stayed with me all the way to the emergency room. The trouncing left me with *another* concussion and *another* contusion. Doctors ordered me to stay overnight for testing and evaluation.

Thankfully, God was still in the business of protecting fools and babies.

Donny came by the hospital after the rodeo finished.

"What could I have done differently?" I asked, looking for his insight and approval. I knew with his years of experience he would have something profound to say. Every bull was a new learning experience. If I had made a mistake, hearing about it from the best was welcomed.

"Nothing," he said. "You did your job right. You saved that cowboy. And that's what we're paid to do."

While subtle and pointed, those were encouraging words from my hero.

Jamie spent what was to be our honeymoon in the Park County Hospital. Not exactly how this cowboy wanted to introduce the sport of rodeo to my new bride. But what better way for her to realize that rodeo is a game of inches? It's not a matter of *if*, but *when* a cowboy gets hurt.

COWBOY LOGIC

1. Is there anything in your life that you know is keeping you from being close to God?

2. How do you deal with professional envy or politics?

3. Track back one answered prayer to its origins.

And we know that in all things God works for the good of those who love Him, who have been called according to His purpose.

Romans 8:28 (NIV)

chapter 10
ONE LAST RODEO

Principle No. 9: Find Your Spotter—Listen to Smart People

Rodeo remained my passion as Jamie and I began building our life together, but the politics and physical toll were starting to get old.

As the concussions and other injuries mounted, routine doctor appointments often turned into career counseling sessions. The wear and tear, they told me, eventually would take some of the shine off my golden years. One doctor even recommended I fight bulls in a helmet to lessen future blows to the noggin. Perhaps it was time to start thinking about other passions.

While I didn't particularly appreciate the unsolicited advice, it was the first indication that God was starting to use people to reveal to me a *new* dream.

It was also the foundation of what I call the Find Your Spotter principle. As a rodeo cowboy prepares to ride a bucking bull or bronc, a trusted friend is always readily available to "spot" the rider. The spotter's protection and advice is vital as the rider gets situated for the ride.

I've never considered myself the smartest person in the room, but the Spotter principle is a friendly reminder that I should always consider the advice of smart people.

AN EAST COAST SWING

My rodeo schedule was full during our second year of marriage. We focused a lot on traveling east to the First Frontier Circuit. Primarily, it was a last-ditch effort to rodeo for the love of the sport. But it also was an opportunity to reach a new market of western enthusiasts.

On the East Coast, rodeo felt more like an American pastime and less like a cutthroat business. Despite flying into Philadelphia International and not knowing a soul, strangers were always willing to lend a hand. Turns out, there are cowboys and cowgirls in the north. Who knew?

In many ways, the strategy worked. It reminded me of the years I longed to get to Cruces early, as if the rodeo couldn't start without me and my Mammaw. Dreaming of being a cowboy. Fighting bulls because I loved it.

At the end of the season, I was selected for the First Frontier Circuit Finals Rodeo. It was a nice accomplishment, especially being voted by bull riders who didn't really know me. But I could tell that the once-sizzling fire was starting to grow dim. I had begun to think more about Jamie and our future than about planning for another rodeo.

In terms of age and ability, I was in my prime—31 years old, in that sweet spot where wisdom and experience intersected with fitness and youth. But working out, an activity that once kept me sane, had become a forced, yet mindless motion. And for the first time, my thoughts were focused more on *my* safety than mitigating risks and saving cowboys. In a sport that requires laying down your life, physical abilities won't save you from injury if the mind and heart aren't fully committed.

Sponsors and money were the primary things keeping me in the game. I knew the doctors had a legitimate point about my health. And I knew my passion for the sport was beginning to fade. But letting it go would be very, very hard.

I needed God to show me the next step in my journey—a step that for the first time might not include rodeo. And what did God do? He literally birthed a new vision for my future.

DOUBLE TROUBLE 2.0

One August morning, Jamie woke up feeling a little queasy. We figured it was just a passing 24-hour bug, so we got ready for work as usual. I put on my uniform and headed to see Uncle Sam. Jamie, working for AT&T, put on her business attire and headed to her office.

As the day progressed, I didn't think too much about it. No news was good news. But then: Ding! Ding! Ding! Three text messages lit up my phone. Each one included a photo of a different pregnancy test. Before I could even get a look, Jamie sent another message saying, "I'm pregnant!"

"Where are you?" I replied. As soon as she said, "At the house," I rushed home. Immediately, I picked up one of the tests she had laid on the bathroom vanity. There they were. Two ever-so-pink lines.

In the moment, both overcome with emotion, we couldn't comprehend the pregnancy test instructions! The instructions were simple diagrams. I'm sure a child could have interpreted them. For the life of me, I couldn't! Did one line mean pregnant, or was it two lines?

We read and reread the instructions. It *appeared* that two faint lines meant we were expecting. But the instructions didn't say which question the test was answering: Were we supposed to have the perspective of, "Are we not expecting?" Or was the question, "Are we expecting?"

I've never been so confused!

Sure I could launch a nuclear missile, but reading a two dollar, color-coded, pregnancy test was a different story! That's a fact.

Not knowing exactly what to do, and seeking validation, we decided to go to the base clinic. The blood work done there confirmed that we were expecting—approximately seven weeks along. Having noticed some spotting, the doctor ordered an ultrasound. The test would reveal great hope or devastating news.

The nurse tried to make small talk as Jamie situated herself on the exam table. We were both too nervous to speak.

When the ultrasound transducer touched Jamie's belly, the nurse started up again.

"Were y'all trying to get pregnant?" she asked.

We eventually wanted children. I definitely wanted the opportunity to be an involved father. But we weren't *trying* to get pregnant.

On the other hand, as Jamie told the nurse, "Well, we weren't trying to *not* get pregnant."

I tried to keep calm, propping against the wall while holding Jamie's hand.

"Were you taking any fertility drugs?" the nurse asked.

"No, ma'am," Jamie replied.

The nurse continued to move the transducer.

After a brief pause she asked Jamie her age followed by the bombshell question: "Do multiples run in your family?"

At this point, I worried that my fainting spells from the mid-90s might return.

"Are we expecting triplets or something?" I asked.

"Close," the nurse replied. "Twins!"

"Sweet Jesus!" I said enthusiastically.

Jamie turned white as the bed sheets, squeezed my hand like a vice grip, and blurted out, "You've got to be kidding me!"

I knew Donny and Ronny as "Double Trouble," so I guess we were having Double Trouble 2.0!

I realized my next purpose in life: I was to be the best husband and dad imaginable. Jamie was going to need me. The twins were going to need me. Our closest family lived in Arkansas, 1,200 miles away. And, even though we had each other, we felt strangely alone.

LETTING GO

The rodeo lifestyle gets in your blood. My Grandpa Sparks was a cowboy drifter. Like him, I loved few things as much as roaming freely from town to town. Even with the fire fading, rodeo still ran through my veins.

Plus, I was still able and healthy. The injuries—multiple concussions, contusions, broken legs, arm, ribs, fingers, and a cracked cheek and tail bone—were just part of the sport. In comparison, two of my friends had been paralyzed and a few peers had suffered broken necks and backs. So I felt fortunate.

Now that we were starting a family, however, Jamie didn't want me to run the risk of getting hurt…or worse. And I certainly didn't want the twins to feel pressure to follow in my footsteps.

Having spent nearly every day of my adult life working to fulfill my childhood dream, I was happy with my career. Furthermore, I felt my particular mission was complete. God had called me to witness, encourage, serve, and testify to a specific demographic, yet now my most important audience would arrive in eight short months.

But how do I walk away from the one thing that has consumed my life?

A piece of me wanted to hang on. Naturally, I would miss rodeo. I would miss seeing my friends. I would miss the freedom found traveling the rodeo circuit.

Retiring certainly went against what the flesh would advise. I was in peak shape, holding multi-year rodeo contracts to a few of the best rodeos in the country. National sponsorships were in hand and I was making 30 percent more money by walking to the mailbox than I was fighting bulls.

On the other hand, I couldn't wait to call it a career. The passion I had as a 14-year-old kid, knowing this was what I was called to do with my life…somewhere between there and here I had lost the desire to sacrifice for rodeo.

Fighting bulls for any reason other than passion, I thought, was doing it for the wrong reason.

I think this is true for everyone, in any profession—if your heart's not in it, you're wasting your time, energy, and potential. But letting go sometimes can be hard to do. Vince Lombardi once said, "The harder that you work, the harder it is to surrender." Even though I knew retiring was the right thing to do, I related to Coach Lombardi's statement.

Throughout the process, Jamie's counsel and wisdom were key as I came to terms with retiring. Without her, I don't know if I could have walked away on my own terms. She was a true helpmate as we prayed through the very hard decision. And after much prayer, I found peace. It was my time to ride off into the sunset.

SAYING GOODBYE

Jamie and I agreed it was only fitting that I return the following rodeo season for a final performance. One last rodeo. I owed it to my sponsors, fans, and to myself.

The twins were due in May, so I let all of my rodeo contracts go prior to the 2010 season, except the two summer rodeos I had grown to love the most: Cheyenne Frontier Days (CFD) and the College National Finals Rodeo (CNFR).

Both were in Wyoming—the CNFR in June and CFD in July—and I wanted to make a Wyoming event my last rodeo. Wyoming Tourism had been a really good sponsor. It was my way to thank them for the years of support.

Now I just had to decide which of those two would be best for my final performance. I could have fought bulls at both, but if I was going to truly hang it up, I felt I needed to make a hard stop.

CFD had launched my rodeo career and put me on the rodeo map. In the 120 years of CFD, I was the only bullfighter who hadn't previously been a world champion or National Finals Rodeo bullfighter. As the multi-time PRCA Large Outdoor Rodeo of the Year, it's simply the best in the world.

The CNFR was also special. It's a great rodeo with great people and a national title on the line. Although Mr. John Smith was no longer the commissioner, I felt a debt of gratitude was owed to him and to college rodeo. Mr. John took a chance on me in 1995 when he offered me a rodeo scholarship during his coaching tenure at McNeese State and again in 2005, signing me on to fight bulls at the CNFR.

How can I possibly choose? I thought.

After careful consideration and working with both the CFD committee and the CNFR directors, I decided the first performance of CFD 2010 would be my last rodeo.

It was a bittersweet decision, but it felt like a massive weight was lifted off my shoulders. The thought of retiring had never entered my mind the first 17 years, but it consumed the last two years of my career. Somewhere along the way, rodeo had transformed from being my life's passion to being a job.

On Thursday, February 25, 2010, I released a written statement to the PRCA announcing my decision.

> *After fighting bulls 10 years in the Professional Rodeo Cowboys Association, I have decided Cheyenne Frontier Days on July 24 will be my lone performance of 2010 and ultimately the final event of my career.*
>
> *I have dedicated over half my life to bullfighting and have never imagined life without rodeo. However, I am confident the time has come for me to walk away from the sport that I love. As a teen from an Arkansas town of 150 people daydreaming about performing on the world's grandest stages, I can honestly say my career has been a journey far exceeding my wildest childhood expectations. Despite the fact that I am still young and able to perform at the highest level, my priorities in life have simply changed and the burning desire to continually put rodeo at the forefront of my life has grown dim.*
>
> *Jamie and I will welcome twin boys to our family this spring, and my goals are to simply be the best dad and family man possible. Due to the rigors of professional rodeo, extensive travel, and my growing desire to enjoy each and every stage of our children's lives, the decision to retire will ensure my priorities don't compete for valuable time.*
>
> *The memories made from all over the world will remain vivid throughout my lifetime, and I want to thank each person who contributed to my success. Whether it was performing at Cheyenne or for heads of state, being in print ads or television campaigns, they are all experiences that I hold dear and prove that even small town kids have big time potential.*
>
> *To God be the glory for giving me the unique ability to do such an extraordinary and dangerous sport while being*

blessed with health and safety that can only come from above.

To my family for standing behind me despite the risks involved and for being my biggest fans.

To my sponsors for supporting me along the route, I will forever be grateful for your belief in me to represent your brand. The United States Air Force and my chain of command, Wrangler, Bailey Hats, Twisted X Boots, Bresnan Communication, and the great State of Wyoming, I sincerely appreciate your trust.

I'd also like to thank professional bullfighters Donny and Ronny Sparks and Mike Matt for inspiring, mentoring, and molding me throughout my rodeo journey. But most importantly I'm indebted to my wife, Jamie, for carrying our twins and allowing me the opportunity to be the best family man I can be.

My parents were thrilled to see me live my passion and equally excited that I was walking away healthy. They had witnessed all the work I had put into accomplishing my God-given dream. They knew that despite the risks and dangers, God had used me in ways that I could have never imagined and taught me life principles I may not otherwise have learned.

Mom emailed me shortly after reading the press release: "Momma is so proud of you. Most people do not pursue their childhood dreams with the passion that you have. Always remember that Momma loves you."

COMPLICATED ARRIVALS

Jett and Jude were born April 9, 2010, just a few feet away from where Jas was born five years prior!

Standing in the Cheyenne Regional Medical Center, I felt the same unexplainable and overwhelming joy. Pride covered every inch of my tall, lanky frame.

This time, I made a promise in the delivery room as I heard their innocent cries for the first time. Like Jesus' love for us, I promised myself and those two little fellows that nothing was going to separate me from my twins. Not rodeo, not Uncle Sam, not in-laws, not anything.

All along, I knew Jamie would need me fully engaged, and not just when I wasn't rodeoing. She and I needed to become the Dynamic Duo to raise Double Trouble 2.0! When Jamie experienced near-fatal complications while in delivery, however, it appeared I might once again be alone.

We had planned for a natural birth, but Jamie went into shock moments prior to fully dilating. As the trauma set in, her body started to shut down. A five-person team made up of doctors and nurses rushed her in for an emergency C-section. The stress caused the twins' blood pressure to drop dangerously low.

It had already been a trying pregnancy, which included a medical flight to Denver Children's Hospital at 31 weeks to stop pre-term labor.

Their lives were at risk.

Standing behind a drop cloth, I held Jamie's hand as she went in and out of consciousness. The medical team worked diligently to deliver the twins. My body was paralyzed with fear, yet I prayed continuously that God would work a miracle before our very eyes.

Then I heard the sweet voice of Twin A. We had named them in the womb, so I knew that cry was Jett. He had his mother's pipes and made a grand entrance, crying at the top of his lungs. I caught a glimpse of him as a doctor handed him over to be cleaned up and swaddled.

The medical team started to work more frantically as they tried to deliver Twin B. One doctor gave the orders, and the team followed his direction with blind obedience. It was very tense. I clung to Jamie's hand and prayed that God was still in the miracle business. In that moment, I was helpless and humbled. As I held Jamie's hand, God held us in His.

After what felt like an hour, two minutes had finally passed. Overhearing the team's conversation, I knew Twin B had been freed from the womb. However, there was no cry. I peeked over the drop cloth hoping to catch a glimpse. To my shock, Jude was blue and unresponsive. Jamie's motherly instincts kicked in.

"Is he okay?" she mumbled.

I couldn't lie. I knew the truth. He wasn't okay.

"God is in control," I said while holding fast to the only hope I knew.

Within a few moments, Jude let out the sweetest whimper! It was amazing to hear his cry and know he was responsive.

The nurses took the twins and me to the nursery. As they started IVs and oxygen, I watched over them like an eagle looking over its nest.

Jett and Jude stabilized nicely despite their early struggle, but Jamie took longer to recover.

When I was reunited with her an hour after she had given birth, she lay motionless, as white as a ghost. Thinking that the touch or sound of the boys would wake her, the nurses carefully transported the twins to Jamie's room.

She wasn't able to sneak a peek during delivery, so it was a breathtaking moment to hand the boys to their mom. But the medications and the trauma had left her unresponsive.

She had given me two perfect boys, but it appeared at times the sacrifice was going to be her life. For four days, she struggled—receiving blood transfusion after blood transfusion. There were major complications with blood not properly clotting and her placenta not discharging. It was gruesome to watch the doctors repetitively scrape to remove the placenta and dislodge the blood clots. I had never seen anything like it. After a week of fighting, it was sweet relief to finally hear the doctors say Jamie was out of the woods.

FAREWELL PERFORMANCE

In the five years since Jas' birth, my priorities had shifted 180 degrees. The thought of being away from the twins and Jamie was gut wrenching. Even thinking about my last event, I knew I had made the right decision to call it a career after one farewell performance.

I could say "goodbye, and thank you" with one lone show. Working an entire event would have meant more interviews, more commitments, and simply more time away from home. And being away from my family wasn't an option.

On July 24th, Jamie brought Jett and Jude to Frontier Park. I'd made the boys miniature Wrangler bullfighting outfits, complete with sponsor patches.

My in-laws made the trip to Cheyenne to witness firsthand the close of our rodeo chapter. What an overwhelming feeling to have the support of my family and in-laws. It was a celebration we all enjoyed.

That morning, we woke up and read the cover story on the *Wyoming Tribune Eagle*. "One Last Rodeo" was printed in huge block letters above an article that began, "Cheyenne bullfighter Jeremy Sparks will walk away from his life's passion after today's rodeo."

Media outlets wanted to interview me, fans wanted to thank me, and sponsors wanted to bid farewell.

All the while, I simply wanted to finish on top. I wanted one more good bullfighting performance, this time for myself. Just once more, I wanted to experience being a vessel for God, letting the light shine so others could see God's love and protection as I shot a gap to serve a fellow man.

Working alongside my mentor and friend, Mike Matt, we did just that for my ninth, and his seventh consecutive year at the "Daddy of 'Em All."

World Champion Bull Rider Wesley Silcox was making his escape for safety as a mean white bull with black spots and big horns turned to charge him.

As the bull zeroed in on Silcox, instinct kicked in once again. Coming from the left side, I shot the gap, positioning myself in between the rider and the raging bull. Neither Wesley nor I were harmed. That's all I wanted, just to serve and protect one last guy— to make one more perfect save.

When the rodeo performance was over, Mike and I returned to the dressing room to clean up and shoot the breeze. I thanked him for the miles and memories.

"This is the apex of your career," Mike said. "Enjoy it and always remember it."

Without God and a number of key people, my career would have certainly looked different. Mike was one of those key people, and it was great to work my last show with him.

I'd come a long way from our Summer 1999 campaign to 2010—I'd covered a lot of miles, seen a lot of the world, improved a lot as a bullfighter, learned a lot as a man, and made a lot of memories. And yes, my fair share of mistakes.

Scanning the dressing room once more, I gathered up my gear bag for the final time.

It was finished.

God had been so good to me. He kept me healthy in a game of inches and I was walking out—on top, on my terms—headed to the next chapter of life.

Jamie, Jett, and Jude were just outside of the locker room waiting for me. I made a silent vow as I shut the dressing room door—I would never return to rodeo.

There wasn't a comeback story in my future. I had left it all on the dirt—the blood, sweat, and tears—it all fell.

COWBOY LOGIC

1. Who's your spotter?

2. How do you help "spot" others?

3. What have you done to thank your spotter?

Where there is no guidance, a people falls, but in an abundance of counselors there is safety.

Proverbs 11:14 (ESV)

chapter 11

REPACKING MY RUCKSACK

Principle No. 10: Turn 'Em Out—Restoration Leads
to Fulfillment

My story wouldn't be complete without revealing my "aha lesson." God used me to encourage and influence people throughout my career, but it wasn't until I learned this lesson that I could fully embrace His calling on my life.

After 17 years of sacrifice, overcoming electrical shock, setbacks, disappointments, despair, and divorce, this is it—the Turn 'Em Out principle. I believe that forgiveness is paramount to fulfillment, and fulfillment isn't possible without restoration.

Back at the C&C Rodeo, we'd often yell, "Turn 'em out!" before a bull ride or bullfight would start. It is rodeo's version of "ready, set, go."

You might think it's about that moment when you spring into action and take control of life, but the principle's application in my life actually signifies letting go. In that moment, a cowboy throws caution to the wind and simply lets go. Training and instinct take over.

To thrive requires letting go and relying on preparation. To survive, it's letting go and trusting God. To stand up after getting knocked down, it's letting go of busted pride.

Letting go often wasn't easy for me.

For years, I internalized and held fast to certain hurts and frustrations. From petty annoyances to major crises, I carried many along the way. These struggles hindered me, lingering deep in my soul. During these times, though I still continued to witness and encourage, it often was hard to feel the prompting, much less obey the call.

Uncle John Allen frustrated me when I began rodeoing. His pleasure seemed to come from my rocky start—and that boggled my mind.

Falling short of my self-imposed goals cut me deep early in my professional career. I just knew satisfaction would be obtained when I reached another milestone or earned a higher title.

Frustrating, too, were the business shenanigans with guys who stood behind the Bible, but lived like the devil. Jealousy and envy made grown men act like spoiled, entitled children.

Divorce was the devil and losing Jas was a dagger to my core. A piece of me was lost forever when that plane took my son across the Atlantic Ocean. He was just a baby. My baby.

There I was, a guy appearing to have life by the tail while simultaneously struggling to make sense of my world. At times, I became distracted by the glitz and glamour of success and lost focus of my mission.

Other times, I was laser-focused, determined to fulfill my calling. The pendulum swung constantly. Seldom did I find the middle ground. While I don't know how fans perceived me, internally, it seemed I was either hot or cold, high or low, on track or distracted.

It was my Uncle Ronnie—my dad's brother—who helped me embrace this value of letting go.

One winter while visiting him in North Carolina, we got on the topic of life. Uncle Ronnie was a Christian and a Vietnam veteran. He was full of practical life experiences and blue-collar philosophy. He shared his wisdom using the art of storytelling, which he had mastered. The parables were real life and applicable, not theory or conceptual ideology.

"Humor me, if you will," Uncle Ronnie said as he began taking our conversation deeper. "On a 40-mile ruck march, carrying over 70 pounds of gear for the love of country, it doesn't matter the distance you have to travel. All you have to do is make it one more step."

He paused, then added, "You've got to make sure and only pack what you need, because 70 pounds gets heavy over time."

He, too, had made some pretty unique choices in life and knew firsthand what it was like to carry hurt, anger, and frustration. Uncle Ronnie saw right through my tough exterior and the accolades I often hid behind.

He continued.

"Have you ever thought about forgiving your Uncle John Allen?"

"No," I swiftly said.

Despite Uncle Ronnie's authenticity and genuine concern, I wasn't much open for discussing the issue.

"You know your Uncle John Allen is a good man," he said.

"Yeah," I mumbled, trying to avoid the conversation. All the while I thought, *What's it matter to you? Y'all aren't blood kin.*

Sure, I knew he was a good guy. I just never let go of how his pleasure in my hookings impacted me in those early rodeo days.

Uncle Ronnie pressed on.

"Next time you are at home, you need to stop by and see him."

What for? I thought.

Uncle Ronnie knew that the only way to stop carrying hurt, anger, frustration, and disappointment was to unload it. To be free, I needed to remove the unnecessary pounds from my rucksack that often weighed me down.

While I didn't feel the need to drive to Arkansas unannounced, I decided to forgive Uncle John Allen. I didn't even call him. I simply let go.

It wasn't a spectacular moment. There wasn't any crying or condolences—just me kneeling at the side of my bed, confessing to God that I was choosing to live in love and let go of past hurts.

In time, I forgave those people in the business who stood behind the Bible, but didn't live by it. Cutthroats, backstabbers, and cowards—I forgave them all.

Forgiveness was the key to my joy, not a rodeo title. My purpose couldn't be fulfilled while simultaneously harboring ill will.

But not all situations were easy to forgive. The divorce and losing Jas were near fatal. Making "just one more step" after losing Jas was excruciating. I battled the thought of him being raised by parents who didn't get along. *Which is worse*, I wondered, *parents separated by emotion or by distance?*

There isn't a right answer. Divorce is gut wrenching.

Not a day goes by that I don't think about Jas. It took years, but I forgave Kriszti and her dad. I even embraced Jas' new name. Now, we all call him Korci, much like a sweet nickname assigned to a small child. He also likes Koko, which is short for Kornél.

Kriszti and I are now able to communicate openly about his health and welfare. Trust me, it wasn't always that way. But with God, all things are possible. After we both unloaded the weight of anger and blame, she shared with me that, "It was like I got a friend back."

Even in a bitter divorce, forgiveness brought freedom.

When I learned to forgive, my fulfillment was no longer tied to a goal, a person, or an event. I'd known all along that my identity was in Christ. However, my rucksack was often loaded with needless weight.

At times, it seemed too much to bear. My back was stooped and my head was low. The thief lingered, looking to kill, steal, and destroy.

I promised Uncle Ronnie that I would keep marching, focusing on just one more step. He helped me repack my rucksack and taught me to live in freedom. Double portions of joy, peace, self-control, love, humility, and kindness needed to be added to my sack.

Along the journey, it became easier to forgive. Granted, I had to remind myself regularly that my own sins had been forgiven. Carrying guilt was counterproductive.

It's hard to lean forward while looking back.

I made a ton of bad choices, yet Psalm 103:12 offered great hope: "As far as the east is from the west, so far has He removed our transgressions from us." (NIV)

I'm not proud of everything in my past, having sinned with the best of them. But looking back and living in regret is guilt, a trick the devil employs to stop us from doing the will of God. Even my darkest shortcomings, I had to Turn 'Em Out.

BEING A VESSEL

When I let go of the unnecessary weight in my rucksack, God was able to better use me to live out the calling He had given me all those years earlier.

Regardless of whether I'd performed well, or the weather condition, or if I was tired, hungry, or hurt—I deliberately made myself available to witness, encourage, serve, and testify. And as I traveled to six countries, more than 40 states, and hundreds of cities, God consistently put people in my path.

My job was simple: To let go and be a vessel God could use.

It was a privilege to meet fine folks from all over the world… to simply be a light on a hill reaching a largely rural demographic. Encouraging fans, family, friends, and complete strangers brought great joy.

Some of them suggested I become a preacher or chaplain. That was not my calling, and besides, my life didn't necessarily scream preacher material. While I was flattered, my ministry was unique, and my approach largely informal.

Fans often shared their aspirations and life goals. It was important to listen and encourage others to live their dream, just as I was living mine.

Military guys in particular sought me out.

"How in the world did you get an endorsement with the Air Force?" they often asked.

While not all were rodeo cowboys, they were passionate about a niche sport. My go-to line was always, "If God can do it for me, He can do it for you."

Traveling the rodeo circuit by plane brought numerous unique moments to encourage strangers and share the Gospel.

While I often longed to go on a traditional mission trip, that wasn't God's plan. My profession was a mission field. So, before every flight, I prayed, "May today be the day I get to be the hands and feet of Jesus." Without fail, God placed people in seats beside and around me who needed to hear an encouraging word or about the love of Jesus.

On one international flight, a middle-aged Asian businessman and I shared an armrest. He was dressed in a fine suit and clung to a designer briefcase. As we made small talk, he revealed the contents of the black leather case. To my surprise, it was filled with Rolex watches—a dozen of those beauties—each cradled in a velvet-lined case. As he showed me the collection, he said, "Not even these watches have brought me happiness."

I jokingly thought, *Would giving me one bring you happiness then?* Before long, I was sharing my testimony. I even had the Bible out reading scripture and walking him through the plan of salvation. We sang "Amazing Grace" to celebrate his newfound knowledge of Jesus.

Not even a finely made Rolex can fill the void of God's love.

Although I preferred to fly, I did my fair share of driving. I even hitchhiked a few times for the thrill. One November day, I arrived at Denver International Airport ahead of schedule. My good friend and frequent traveling partner, Ira McKillip, was scheduled to pick me up. For whatever reason, I was early and he was delayed.

I thought, *Shoot, I can walk home by the time Ira gets here.*

So I did.

With my cowboy hat on, a gear bag strapped across my shoulder and suitcase in tow, I headed to the EZ-470 toll road. It was Cheyenne or bust. Just as I was nearing the toll road, a Chevy Sonic pulled over. Two elderly ladies reluctantly offered me a ride.

"We haven't met a cowboy before," the driver said.

"We're from the Bronx, New York," added the passenger.

"Interesting," I replied. "Well, now you have!"

"I'm Jeremy Sparks, a cowboy from L.A. and an officer in the Air Force."

"L.A.?" they asked.

"Yes, Lower Arkansas!"

The joke broke the ice, and we shared our first laugh.

"Can I offer you any gas money?" I asked while reaching for my wallet. They insisted that their safety was the only payment acceptable. Sounded like a plan to me. I wasn't carrying a gun, but I can now see that reaching for my pocket wasn't the brightest move.

As I tried to get situated in the small car, the passenger asked, "Now, who do you say you are again?"

"I'm Jeremy Sparks," I assured her.

"And what is it you say you do?"

"I'm a rodeo bullfighter."

"And you say that you're in the Air Force?"

"Yes, ma'am."

Other than being open for a good story, I have no idea why I hitchhiked to Cheyenne that day. I'm not sure why those ladies helped a complete stranger, either. But I do know that I shared my story over the next 90 miles.

If God could love me, He could certainly love them, too.

Perhaps one of the most profound examples of being a vessel for Christ happened in a locker room as I was preparing for the College National Finals Rodeo.

More than a decade prior in Little Rock, I sat in amazement listening to Rick Chapman, Leon Coffee, and Jeff Grigsby tell rodeo stories as they autographed pictures for me. Leon's encouraging words that day made a lasting impression on me. As my career evolved, Leon and I worked numerous events together, including my first circuit finals rodeo. I was no longer starstruck. We were simply rodeo peers.

It was the first day of the CNFR.

Leon had driven all night from his home in Texas to Casper, Wyoming. He was exhausted. Lounging and relaxing in the dressing room, we laughed and traded stories from the trail.

He also shared that his dad's health had recently declined. I felt for him. His mind was clearly on family, and he felt stuck nearly 1,200 miles from home.

Leon had no more finished talking about his dad when his phone rang.

I sat quietly and continued to lay out my bullfighting gear. Leon listened intently to the voice on the other end. Then, his face started to melt. Clearly, it was one of those calls you never want to get.

His body began to shake.

Tears fell from his face, and Leon cried out, "No, no, no."

His heart was broken as he hung up the phone. Collapsing onto the bright-yellow countertop, he put his head in his hands and wept.

Like any friend would, I went to his side and embraced him.

"Sparks," he said, "Daddy's gone."

There were no words in my vocabulary for the situation. My parents were still alive. I hadn't experienced that same hurt, and I certainly didn't have the right words to say.

"Can I pray with you?" I quietly asked.

That was all I knew to do. And that's what we did. As two grown men representing the toughest personnel in rodeo, we hugged, we grieved, and I prayed that God would provide peace and comfort to my friend.

I believe it was God's divine plan for Leon not to be alone in that moment. I was merely the person placed in his path.

Divine appointments and Holy Spirit promptings are absolute. The obedience to be used by God in such moments is a choice.

We can accept them, or we can ignore them.

My greatest satisfaction is looking back and seeing how God used a small-town kid—essentially a nobody—to influence and encourage others for His good. To a certain degree, we leave a little of ourselves with everyone we encourage—exhortation DNA, or XDNA, if you will.

I certainly have carried Donny Sparks' XDNA with me throughout my life. Never once did I forget the example Donny instilled in me that day at the Four States ProRodeo, so many moons ago.

"Be kind and encourage others," he said.

Throughout the journey, everyone needs encouragement. The God of the universe calls each of us to a specific purpose: "For we are God's handiwork, created in Christ Jesus to do good works, which God prepared in advance for us to do." (Ephesians 2:10, NIV)

What if you are the one person who offers the right word to the right person at the right time to help them pursue their God-given dream? Matthew 25:40 says these opportunities will come. They are a privilege, not an obligation: "Truly I tell you, whatever you did for one of the least of these brothers and sisters of mine, you did for me." (NIV)

You never know who God will put in your path.

FINDING REDEMPTION

The heart of my message to others includes this basic truth: We are all broken people.

The Bible says sin caused our brokenness. It comes in many shapes and often presents itself as pleasure: addiction, greed, pride, worry, sexual immorality, etc. It all leads to separation from God.

The Bible says we all have sinned and fallen short of the glory of God (Romans 3:23). God, in his infinite wisdom and unconditional love, sent His only son, Jesus, to die on the cross for our sins (John 3:16). He was raised to life three days later, defeating death, and ascended into heaven. At this very moment, He sits at the right hand of the Father (1 Corinthians 15:4, Acts 7:55), making it possible for you and I to become worthy before the Lord God Almighty.

Jesus' death and resurrection were solely for me and you—so that we may have restoration and fulfillment. He was pierced for our transgressions and raised for our justification (Isaiah 53:5).

Forgiveness is offered to broken people from a perfect Savior, so that we may have eternal life. All we have to do is repent and accept Jesus as the Son of God. His grace, mercy, love, and forgiveness await all those who believe. The Bible promises in Matthew 7:8, "For everyone who asks receives; the one who seeks finds; and to the one who knocks, the door will be opened." (NIV)

Don't be fooled by what the world says.

We will never be good enough or do enough to earn God's love. It is a free gift rooted in what Jesus did on the cross. Ephesians 2:8-9 testifies, "For by grace you are saved through faith, and this is not of yourselves, it is the gift of God; it is not of works, so that no one can boast." (ESV)

Being a good person, a hard worker, a trusted friend, an accomplished businessman, a straight-A student, a child prodigy, or a world champion will not get us to heaven. In John 14:6, Jesus states, "I am the way, and the truth, and the life. No one comes to the Father except through me." (ESV)

Do you believe this truth? It's simple, yet profound.

It is life changing. Are you willing to repack your rucksack?

Jesus says in Matthew 11:30, "For my yoke is easy, and my burden is light." (ESV)

Fulfillment isn't possible without restoration. Complete restoration only comes from a relationship with Jesus Christ. It cannot be known apart from the Lord. "But to all who did receive him, who believed in His name, He gave the right to become children of God," says John 1:12. (ESV)

Like you, I was created in the image of God, with a sense of purpose and a burning desire to "Go West." The great news is, God has blessed each individual—no matter the race, color, physical ability, or social status—with a gift, a passion, a burning desire.

But it isn't until we find out *why* that we will find out *how*.

COWBOY LOGIC

1. Who do you need to forgive?

2. What does brokenness look like in your life?

3. Do you accept Jesus Christ as the Son of God and your only hope of salvation?

For God so loved the world that he gave his one and only Son, that whoever believes in him shall not perish but have eternal life.

John 3:16 (NIV)

Epilogue
THE YEARS SINCE

Life outside of rodeo has been more fulfilling than I ever imagined. My faith is still in Jesus, I'm still a cowboy, and I'm still a sinner. I just seldom wear a cowboy hat.

The education my parents and Donny encouraged me to finish allowed for a seamless transition into my next phase of life. I walked out of the arena Saturday afternoon July 24, 2010 as *retired* bullfighter, Jeremy Sparks. On Monday morning July 26, 2010, I was back to being Major Sparks, serving Uncle Sam. In that moment I realized the true value of education and went on to earn my MBA.

In 2013, I left active duty military service to return to Arkansas, starting a career with a Fortune 100 company. Jamie and I wanted the twins to be closer to family as our parents aged. The Air National Guard has been a perfect fit, allowing me to continue my service.

Later that year, I was inducted into the 2013 Class of the Cheyenne Frontier Days Hall of Fame. At 36, I became the youngest person ever enshrined. It was a huge honor to join the likes of Lane Frost, Chris LeDoux, George Strait, Reba McEntire, and many other great cowboys, cowgirls, and entertainers.

While serving on a temporary duty in Oberammergau, Germany, I visited the 18th-century Weis Pilgrimage Church in Steingaden. Standing at the front of the church, I asked God to once again reveal His plans for my life. Despite being 5,000 miles from home, I was still in the presence of God. Just as He spoke to me as a teenager, He answered my prayer.

"Worship Me!" He said.

While my rodeo days are over, I continue to *Go West*.

MY BRIDE AND KIDS

Jamie and I are still the Dynamic Duo wrangling Double Trouble 2.0. She's just as beautiful and outgoing as ever and supports my every move. She's learned to appreciate the dreamer in me, and I certainly value her attention to details.

She's my soulmate and we've continued exploring the United States, from Alaska to Florida. We look forward to growing old together and providing the boys with the resources to help them fulfill their dreams.

Kornél still lives in Hungary with his mom. He's a gifted athlete and loves soccer. At 11, he is already playing in the Elite Labdarúgó Football Academy for the Hungarian National Soccer Team and has twice won Male Athlete of the Year at his school. We FaceTime weekly and spend one week each summer together.

Jett wants to be an astronaut. He loves school and running. He has his Momma's smile—we call him Smiley! I hope my example proves to him that he can do anything he puts his mind to, even reaching outer space.

Jude loves all sports, but wants to be a tennis player. He enjoys recess and has my determination—we call him Mischief! He's a daring little fellow and always the first to jump into the action and bite off more than he can chew.

FAMILY

Momma only came to see me fight bulls three times in my professional career, but she never missed praying before every performance. I continued to call her after every rodeo. I called her from pay phones, stranger's phones, from overseas, and from the backs of ambulances—but I always called my momma!

In 2012, she went to be with the Lord after a brief but courageous battle with cancer. She was 69. I miss her just as badly today as I did the day she passed away.

Dad was a great role model for my brothers and me, modeling servant leadership on a daily basis until he lost his own battle with cancer in July 2016. He was 74. He held my momma tight the three times she watched me rodeo, including keeping her sane after witnessing a bull kick me in the face in 2004. He was a prayer warrior, and I try to mimic his Christian walk. I've never met a better man.

My brother Jeff continues to operate his small business in Marvell, Arkansas. His support was vital to my career. From financing my first protective vest, to paying for my PRCA evaluation, he supported me in any way he could. I gave him the Circuit Finals buckle I earned in 2008, and it's still proudly displayed in his home.

Jay, my other brother, lives with his family of five in New Mexico. He's living his dream as a hospital chaplain. He was on hand the weekend I was evaluated by the PRCA. That will always be a great family memory, knowing that he, his wife, and infant son (my first nephew) shared in that milestone moment.

My Mammaw Cruce died in 1999 at age 88. She never got to see me fulfill my destiny of being a professional bullfighter, at least not on this side of heaven. I hope I will allow my kids and grandkids to take risks the way she let me. Had it not been for her support (and ability to keep a secret), I would have needed a Plan B!

Uncle John Allen battled alcoholism and won. In 2005, he and my Aunt Dian came to Cheyenne to watch me fight bulls. He didn't have to do that, but I sure was glad he got to see a product of the C&C Rodeo Company go to 'em in the big pen. He continues the western way of life, touring south Arkansas by mule and wagon. Why? Because he enjoys it. Being a cowboy drifter runs in our blood.

Uncle Jerry and Aunt Sharon are now retired. They raise livestock on the original home place off Midway Route. He still wears spurs every day, even to church. He's a cowboy and will be until the day he dies.

"Cruces" closed in 2004, but not before producing a handful of rodeo stars, including three Professional Bull Riders (PBR) finals qualifiers, and Promise Land, the 1997 PBR Bucking Bull of the Year. Oh, yea, and JIT...he went on to fight at the National Finals Rodeo! Not bad stats for a small arena off an old dirt road.

Aunt Dian keeps the family traditions alive since Mom passed. She and Uncle John Ricks are my financial advisers—we've managed to lose a lot of money together...but the dividend checks are still coming in!

Uncle Ronnie met Jesus in 2012 after battling cancer. Even in that fight, he focused on taking just one more step. He was 68 years old. During our last visit, in his final days, he said, "I love you like a son, and I'm proud of the Christian man you have become." Knowing where I came from, that remains one of the best compliments I've ever received. Presenting the American flag to my Aunt Nancy at his funeral remains one of the most emotional tasks I've ever faced.

The Jordan's (my in-laws) were a Godsend. Big Jack and Momma Jane remain supportive and together serve as a great example of a Godly marriage. Momma Jane played a pivotal role in me adjusting to life after my mom passed. They nod along when I tell them, "I'm their favorite son-in-law!"

Ms. Mary and Mr. Smed will always be my Wyoming family. Smed is 94 years old and going strong. Ms. Mary is still an angel. They are grandparents to our twins. As I travel back to Wyoming to serve in the National Guard, I always stay at their home; in the same room I stayed when I had lost it all.

Kriszti remains in Hungary where she works as a physical education teacher and basketball coach. We work hard to always do what's best for Kornél. I've never gone to sleep worrying about Koko. Without a doubt, she works diligently to be the best mom she can be for him.

Her parents still live in Hungary as well. They support Kornél as he pursues his passion for soccer. Despite our earlier differences, they've come to appreciate the efforts I've made to stay involved in his life. I appreciate them for investing in Kornél.

RODEO FAMILY

Donny Sparks remains my hero. Our relationship has evolved over the years—transitioning from mentor, to peer, to cherished friend. He will always be remembered as the person God chose to solidify my dream. Donny retired in 2008, just one event after we worked the Cody Stampede together.

Ronny Sparks is still "The Champ." The three-time world champion still remains a phone call away. He is tied with Mike Matt as the second most-decorated bullfighter in the world.

Rick Chatman passed away in 2014 as the result of an apparent heart attack. He was 57. We lost touch after he retired from rodeo in 2003. However, I will never forget his support for my career and the great humility he showed by opening the door to CFD.

Cody Martin is still a close friend. He went on from Martin, Tennessee to win the College National Finals Rodeo, earn ProRodeo's Rookie of the Year title, and twice qualify for the National Finals Rodeo. We still laugh about my one day of work at MTD!

Mike Matt married Lesli, a lady we met while rodeoing in Cheyenne. They have a beautiful family: one son and twin girls. Mike retired from bullfighting in 2013, a legend in the sport. We remain close friends and talk frequently.

Art McDaniel walked away from rodeo to focus on his family

and a career in law enforcement. Despite losing contact with him after moving to Wyoming in 2002, I always carried his lessons with me, and I have never smelled a banana without thinking about him!

Ira McKillip is still a character and good friend. He retired from rodeo in 2012 and battled cancer throughout 2015 and since. Over the years, we shared a lot of memories together and look forward to telling old rodeo stories when we're old and gray.

Charlie Sampson is one of the most genuine people I've ever met. In 2013, Charlie surprised me when he walked into the hall of fame banquet after the ceremony had begun. He handed me a card that read, "I wouldn't have missed this for the world."

FRIENDS

James Meeks still owns Meeks Tomato Farm and we all remain family friends. I never returned to the farm after my accident, but I'm certain he still considers me his best farm hand!

Chad Saunders remains a great friend. Since our days conversing at Seldom Rest Ranch, he's had a pretty impressive rodeo career himself. Most recently he's fought cancer and won!

Jonathan Walthall is still one of my best friends. We ended up pledging Pike and rooming together at UCA. We both later graduated from UAM, served at F.E. Warren together, and our wives had twins. We will always be friends.

Matt Williams never pursued a professional rodeo career, as he focused on being a husband and father. His friendship over the years has been vital to my journey. I recall him accepting the Lord as his Savior as if it were yesterday.

Dr. Dennis Travis retired from UAM in 2004. He remained a mentor until his death in September 2011. He was 67.

Sean Graves retired from the United States Air Force in 2012, after 20 years of service, including two combat deployments. In fact, when he left our home following the 9/11 attacks, he was among the first airmen in Afghanistan. As God would have it, I was serving on temporary duty in New Jersey when Sean retired. It was the first time we had seen each other since 2001.

Mr. Lee Jong-Pill with the Korean Ministry of Tourism became a dear friend. In 2008, he and his wife joined me and Jamie at Cheyenne Frontier Days. He brought me to South Korea four times to perform at the Cheongdo Bullfighting Festival, a true highlight in my career.

Lt. Col. James "Jim" Carrol, who initially contacted me about my desire to perform at CFD, went on to make Brigadier General. When he heard about my selection to the CFD Hall of Fame, he wrote me saying, "This is way cool to hear!" His investment in my life will never be forgotten.

Kal Robinson retired from the Air Force in 2007 and relocated to Montana. He is an awesome guy and one of the few people who have seen me at my highest and lowest points in life. There's never been a better friend.

Dr. Travis Plumlee was the mightiest Christian warrior I ever met. Since our time at UCA, he never missed a day praying for me. When he passed away in 2016, he'd prayed for me over 7,000 times. I pray that I can disciple others just as he discipled me.

Jason King is a brother in Christ. Late one night in 2015, I was reading my Bible and God laid it on my heart to pray for him. It was odd, but like driving to the church parking lot, I obeyed.

Around midnight, I sent him a text saying, I have no idea why but God told me to pray for you. He replied, "Brother, you have no idea what this means to me. I'm faced with a challenging situation and to know that God has used you to reach me proves that He is in control."

ACKNOWLEDGMENTS

While it may sound cliché, I must first thank God for breathing life into *Go West*. Everything in this book has been prayed over and revealed through scripture, prayer, and fasting. I thank God for guiding me through this process.

A host of family, friends, and confidants have supported this endeavor, and I am sincerely grateful. Mark Russell and the entire Elevate Publishing team worked tirelessly to make *Go West* a reality. Not having an agent, I pitched my story on a wing and a prayer. Elevate was the first publisher I submitted the proposal to, and Mark stepped out on faith. Thank you.

I also want to thank the *Go West* prayer warriors: My wife, Jamie, my late dad, Elmer Sparks, brothers Jeff and Jay Sparks, in-laws Jack and Jane Jordan, the late Travis Plumlee, Jason King, and the small group couples who meet with Jamie and me faithfully every Wednesday night. Thank you all. In fact, group member Clif Anderson is responsible for introducing me to Stephen Caldwell.

While Stephen originally supported *Go West* in an advisory role and as a content editor, I am forever grateful that he yielded to selflessly help me. Working with a professional author elevated the quality of my writing, resulting in the book that you are now reading. Therefore, it is only right that my new friend is listed on the cover. I've never met a more selfless man. Stephen, you're a Godsend. Thanks, brother!

Justin McKee always made me feel larger than life when introducing me to rodeo crowds over the years. Witnessing him live his faith was an inspiration. I am grateful for his friendship and commitment to write the foreword and help me connect to others in our industry. Thanks, Justin, for carving time out for *Go West*.

When there were merely scribblings on paper, one man and one woman invested time and energy to read, edit, and encourage me to keep on keeping on.

The man: John Pope. You are true friend. Thanks for believing in my story.

The woman: Jamie Sparks. You are a true helpmate. Thanks for the honest and loving feedback; daring me to dig deeper. I couldn't have done this without you.

At the conclusion of my rodeo career, I knew that one day, I wanted to write a book. Simply put, I wanted my kids to have a small glimpse into their dad's life. So, to my boys: Kornél, Jett, and Jude, *Go West* wouldn't have been accomplished without you. Dare to live your dreams. *Szeretlek*.

Tight Squeeze
Coming to the rescue of a bull rider at the historic Cowtown Rodeo in Pilesgrove, New Jersey

Photo by Eva Scofield

ABOUT THE AUTHOR

Photo by Eric Chin

Soon after accepting Jesus Christ into his life, Jeremy Sparks received a specific vision from God. At 14, God called Jeremy to be a rodeo bullfighter. He went on to become a professional bullfighter and was later enshrined in the Cheyenne Frontier Days Rodeo Hall of Fame. Jeremy earned his MBA and served his country as an officer in the Air Force where he was endorsed by the Pentagon as the "only professional bullfighter in the history of the USAF." Jeremy and wife, Jamie, live in Fayetteville, Arkansas with their beautiful twin boys.

Follow JeremySparks_GoWest:

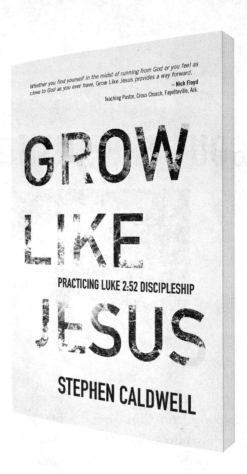

If you enjoyed *Go West* or want to strengthen
your walk with Christ, *Grow Like Jesus* may
be a book for you.

Visit www.elevatepub.com to
place an order today!

elevate
publishing

DELIVERING TRANSFORMATIVE MESSAGES
TO THE WORLD

Visit www.elevatepub.com for our latest offerings.